GW00675778

The Glenstal Book
of Readings
for the Seasons

the columba press

First published in 2008 by
The Columba Press
55A Spruce Avenue, Stillorgan Industrial Park,
Blackrock, Co Dublin

Acknowledgements

Every effort has been made to contact copyright holders and their
permission is acknowledged at the end of each quotation. In the
few cases where we have been unable to trace copyright holders,
the publishers invite them to contact us so that matters can be put
right in future editions.

Designed by Bill Bolger
The cover icon is a 17th-century depiction of Saint Athanasius,
Glenstal Abbey Icon Chapel
Origination by The Columba Press
Printed in Italy by L.E.G.O., Vicenza

ISBN 978-1-85607-580-0

Contents

Preface

From earliest available records, societies on this planet have based their measurement of time, their yearly calendars, on the movements of the Sun and the Moon. Most Western countries now use the Gregorian calendar which was revised, from Julius Caesar's calendar, in 1582. This is based on the Sun and the 365.242 days that the earth takes to circle it.

Hebrew and Muslim calendars are based on the Moon. The first of these is dated from 3761 BC, the year when the earth was supposed to have been created; the second from 622 AD, the year Muhammad moved from Mecca to Medina.

Whichever way we decide to compute, each year is naturally cyclical: Winter, Spring, Summer, Autumn, if we live on certain parts of the planet. Nearer to the equator there is less obvious diversification, but it still comes round again in a circle. We, in our Western world, derive our calendar from the Romans. We begin each year on the 1st of January, named after Janus, the God of gateways, whose festival was celebrated by the Romans at that time of year. July and August are called after Julius Caesar and his successor Caesar Augustus and we even accept that both these months should have thirty-one days because Augustus decided to lengthen his month so that it be not shorter than his predecessor's. To redress the imbalance, he also decreed that February have twenty-eight days. Amazing that these time-shares have survived. You would imagine that our more recent puritanical ancestors would have run a mile from such paganism. But, in truth, running a mile was also a Roman invention. It was the Latin for a thousand and measured a thousand paces. Only at the end of the twentieth century did we take to running in metres.

September to December are the Latin names for seven to ten, *septem, octo, novem*, and *decem*. Until about 150 BC, the Roman year began in March. So, these last months were the seventh, eighth, ninth and tenth months after the beginning of the year in March. Mars was the God of war. April came from the Latin *aperire* meaning to open, because of the unfolding buds and blossoms of spring. May was the goddess of fertility (Maia) and Juno goddess of the Moon. She also begins our week as Monday, the day of the moon. Depending on whether your language is English or one of the related Germanic languages such as German, Dutch, Danish or Swedish, the days of your week will be called after Teutonic or Norse Gods and Goddesses. French and other Romance languages such as Italian and Spanish will derive their weekdays from Classical mythology. Tiw of our Tuesday is a teutonic God identified with Mars [hence the French Mardi as in Mardi Gras]. Wodin or Odin and Thor, God of thunder, from the Nordic pantheon, take care of Wednesday and Thursday. Frigg or Freya and Saturn are in charge for the weekend on Friday and Saturday. We are living in a carefully constructed world encased in pagan time.

Christianity has devised an alternative year, symbolising a different way of living time, which provides those of us who choose to be otherwise, with a liturgical calendar. We insert the mysteries of Christ's life into the seasons and the times of the year, beginning with Advent and carry on to Pentecost, from November to June approximately. This allows us to live these mysteries in ways which give access to the full reality of resurrection. Christianity is not a new religion, it is a new form of existence. It is the introduction of the dimension of resurrection into the spatio-temporal continuum of ordinary daily life.

Resurrection is not some all-powerful divine act. It is rather the visible and tangible effect of the meeting and union of divine love with human being. This connection is the miracle which God has always been trying to effect since the beginning of time and it is the reason why Jesus Christ entered our world. But resurrected life does require of us some adjustment, some rearrangement of the way in which we live. It involves an alternative approach to time. The difficulty is that we are hybrid creatures. Part of us is geared towards such connection but other parts of us are allergic to it.

Resurrection means standing up and moving heavenwards. It can be symbolised by a vertical line, a tree, a totem pole, a steeple. Because this vertical line of resurrection is crossed by the horizontal line of heredity, biology, nature, we are the crossroads for two conflicting ways of living. The way we are by our human birth conflicts with the way we are called to be by resurrection. Such is the intersection we are trying to negotiate, the cross of human existence. Biology fashions us in a way that militates against resurrection; it forms in us a particular will which crosses swords with the 'personal' will of our true spirit, which is formed by the Holy Spirit.

We prefer, naturally, to live like ants or bees with an in-built code of behaviour, a blue-print for conducting our lives. Birth, marriage, death, these are the horizontal way, the natural pattern of human behaviour. So many dictators and perpetrators of ideologies have pandered to such natural tendencies and tried to force us into totalitarian juggernauts of another's design and construction.

As Christians, we are asked to take over the steering wheel and change that natural, horizontal direction. We should be moving upwards in a spiral, marking our progress year by year. The way we do that is by switching over to the alternative energy of divine life. Liturgy makes it possible for us to do this on a daily basis. Nor does this mean that we repudiate what is natural and biological in favour of another, a better, a higher way of being. The principle of incarnation means that we achieve the incorporation of both dimensions into one integrated whole. We move towards the infinite, the divine, the eternal, without damaging one tissue, without spilling one drop of what it means to be fully human, to be fully alive as men and women.

This book provides a daily account of such progress. It accompanies with specially chosen and appropriate readings, the Liturgy of Morning Prayer from Advent to Pentecost. It follows the pattern of our salvation from the arrival of Christ into our lives, through the mysteries of his life, death and resurrection, to the sending of the Holy Spirit at Pentecost. It shows us how we can conform our daily lives to the pattern of his, by making the connection between what he did during his earthly life and what we do every morning of ours.

We have chosen each reading to explain as clearly as possible the particular part of this total mystery which is being celebrated each day of the year. Each reading has been tried and tested at Glenstal Abbey in Ireland where a community of monks assemble for prayer and listen to these readings at seven o'clock every morning. In such circumstances only the deepest and the clearest survive. Only those who can say what it really means in the shortest, simplest and most accessible way, survive the cut. Where they incline to complication or verbosity, they are edited and pruned.

These readings should provide the clearest, simplest and yet most profound interpretation of the height and the depth, the length and the breadth, of those mysteries which make up the saving work of Jesus Christ. These are displayed in our liturgical seasons from the preparation for the arrival of the Second Person of the Trinity in Advent, to the completion of this work in the descent of the Holy Spirit at Pentecost.

'Day unto day takes up the story and night unto night makes known the message' (Psalm 19).

The Season of Advent

First Sunday of Advent

Advent
Patrick Kavanagh

We have tested and tasted too much, lover –
Through a chink too wide there comes in no wonder.
But here in this Advent-darkened room
Where the dry black bread and the sugarless tea
Of penance will charm back the luxury
Of a child's soul, we'll return to Doom
The knowledge we stole but could not use.

And the newness that was in every stale thing
When we looked at it as children: the spirit-shocking
Wonder in a black slanting Ulster hill,
Or the prophetic astonishment in the tedious talking
Of an old fool, will awake for us and bring
You and me to the yard gate to watch the whins
And the bog-holes, cart-tracks, old stables where Time begins.

O after Christmas we'll have no need to go searching
For the difference that sets an old phrase burning –
We'll hear it in the whispered argument of a churning
Or in the streets where the village boys are lurching.
And we'll hear it among simple, decent men, too
Who barrow dung in gardens under trees,
Wherever life pours ordinary plenty.

Won't we be rich, my love and I, and please
God we shall not ask for reason's payment,
The why of heart-breaking strangeness in dreeping hedges,
Nor analyse God's breath in common statement.
We have thrown into the dust-bin the clay-minted wages
Of pleasure, knowledge and the conscious hour –
And Christ comes with a January flower.

Reprinted from *Collected Poems*, edited by Antoinette Quinn
(Allen Lane, 2004) by kind permission of the Trustees of the
Estate of the late Katherine B. Kavanagh, through the Jonathan
Williams Literary Agency.

Monday of the first week of Advent

The Message of Isaiah
Vincent Ryan

During the four weeks of Advent the prophet Isaiah is read.
This is rightly so, since he is the greatest of the messianic
prophets. Isaiah is a man of great vision and deep religious
conviction; these he combines with great power of poetic
expression. Zealous for the honour of God, he is filled with
indignation when God's law is disobeyed. He is not afraid
to castigate his people for their infidelity. There are warn-
ings and reproaches as well as words of comfort and good
tidings. There are oracles against the nations and diatribes
against the people. But underneath all of these there is a
deep current of hope and of joy. Isaiah describes in memor-
able imagery the peace and security of the messianic age.
He looks beyond the afflictions of the present to an era of
universal peace. This new age will be inaugurated by a
Messiah, himself gentle and wise. All the scattered children
of Israel will return from exile. Mount Zion, the Temple,
will become the spiritual centre not only of Israel but of
the whole world. The restoration of the Jewish people is
but a prelude to the restoration of all humankind. God's
plan of salvation does not exclude any race or nation.

Isaiah wrote during the second half of the eighth century
BCE at a time of great national crisis during the Assyrian
invasions of Palestine. The complete Book of Isaiah is an
anthology of poems composed chiefly by the great prophet,
but also by disciples, some of whom came many years after
himself. The ministry of Isaiah may be divided into three

periods, covering the reigns of Jotham (742-735), Ahaz (735-715), and Hezekiah (715-687). To the first period belong, for the most part, the early oracles (Isaiah 1-5) which exposed the moral breakdown of Judah and its capital, Jerusalem. With the accession of Ahaz, the prophet became adviser to the king, whose throne was threatened by the Syro-Ephraimite coalition. Rejecting the plea of Isaiah for faith and courage, the weak Ahaz turned to Assyria for help. From this period came the majority of messianic oracles found in the section of Immanuel prophecies (Isaiah 6-12). Hezekiah succeeded his father and undertook a religious reform which Isaiah undoubtedly supported. But the old intrigues began again, and the king was soon won over to the pro-Egyptian party. Isaiah denounced this 'covenant with death' and again summoned Judah to faith in Yahweh as her only hope.

It was the role of the prophet to lift the spirits of his people, to show the providence of God at work even in the midst of disaster. Assyria acted quickly and her army, after ravaging Judah, laid siege to Jerusalem. 'I shut up Hezekiah like a bird in his cage,' boasts the famous inscription of Sennacherib. But Yahweh delivered the city, as Isaiah had promised: God is the Lord of history, and Assyria but an instrument in his hands. For, if the Lord punishes, he also heals. 'When the Lord has given you the bread of suffering and the water of distress, he who is your teacher will hide no longer, and you will see your teacher with your eyes.'

From *Advent to Epiphany*, Veritas Publications 1982. Used by kind permission of the publisher.

Tuesday of the first week of Advent

The Liturgical Year
Adrian Nocent

If we are to understand the liturgy, we must take as our starting point the incarnation of the Word and the later coming of the Spirit. Until the Word became incarnate, our experience of God was of a philosophical kind: a prayerful reflection, an intellectual and psychological approach to God, with the more or less profound effects this might have on the person's private and social behaviour. The Hebrew Testament, in its steadfast monotheism, shows the beginnings of a mediation through signs, for example, the sign of fire, which indicates the presence of the Lord.

With the incarnation, however, the manner in which we come into saving contact with God is radically changed, and the flesh becomes the instrument of salvation. As soon as we say 'incarnation' we are bound to take past, present, and future into account.

The Past: Christ focuses upon his own person all the expectations and the whole typology of the Hebrew Testament. Christ who is born according to the flesh represents the fulfillment of the Hebrew Testament types, which are neither simple prophecies nor simple examples, but the starting points of events that are fulfilled in Christ and continue to be fulfilled in the church.

The Present: Through signs, we are in contact with Christ who continues to be present. Our experience of God is a sacramental experience. It is an experience that is, so to speak, materialist, being both our own and intrinsically bound up with the incarnation. Only because the body of Christ is glorified is it possible for us to enter into contact, here and now, with all his mysteries. The celebration of Christmas is not a simple remembering: rather, it actualises for us the whole mystery of the incarnation. The expectation that characterises Advent is a genuine, not a simulated, expectation of what Christmas makes real.

The Future: In our liturgical experience of God we are always constructing a future. We are not simply being drawn towards a future; we are building it together with Christ, who is present through us. The entire world has the task of reconstructing itself in view of a future until God's plan is perfectly fulfilled and Christ comes to gather in the mature fruit of his entire work of paschal reconciliation.

From *The Liturgical Year: Advent, Christmas, Epiphany,* Collegeville, MN: The Liturgical Press, 1977. Used by kind permission of the publisher.

Wednesday of the first week of Advent

The Church's Year
Odo Casel

When the church speaks of a 'year' or as the ancients did of a yearly cycle (*anni circulus*) they meant something quite different from our meaning today. The circle is the opposite of all development: as something completely round it is the symbol of eternity, of God.

In the circle there is no before or after, no greater or less; it contains the highest point of likeness and oneness. The circle is an image of life but of life without development, without growth; of eternal life and fullness (*Pleroma*). Circle and sphere are the sensible images of eternal perfection. The sacred course of the liturgy speaks of eternity not of nature, which comes, blooms, puts forth its fruit, then fades and dies. There is no dying in the church year, only life.

Nature has a shadowy eternity in her capacity to come back to life after fading and sinking away; but death always comes again; how short the bloom is, how long the dying and the death. There is no winter in the church's year; if it starts up again, circle forming on circle, this constant return is to suggest the divine quality of the mystery. St Ambrose in one of his morning hymns calls Christ, 'the true day which shines on day, the true Sun which casts everlasting splendour'. Christ is therefore 'the day which is splendid with the light that knows no evening.' Christ is also the true year, whilst the world's day is ending; Christ is Lord of all the seasons. This is not so because he perpetually renews himself, like natural light, but because he is light and life without winter, darkness or decline. In the church year on earth he gives us a mystical reflection of his own everlasting day with God.

From *The Mystery of Christian Worship,* Darton, Longman and Todd 1962. Used by kind permission of the publisher.

Thursday of the first week of Advent

The Mysteries of Christ
Odo Casel

The mysteries of Christ have a two-sided character. In themselves they are divine, yet they mirror temporal action. We live the Lord's year in this world where we experience birth, growth, maturity, suffering and death. His resurrection and ascent to the Father's right hand truly take us across into the kingdom of God. The church year contains so much of the Lord's earthly life that since the end of the late middle ages it has been taken as a spiritual participation and contemplation of that life.

Would this still be a mystery? It would be a moral sharing in the life and feeling of Jesus, but no mystical oneness with the Christ the *Kyrios* in the order of being, not the oneness which, according to his teaching and that of his apostles, is the aim and meaning of Christian life. If that life has its role in the church's year, then the year must have another meaning.

It is not that common life and consciousness with Christ are excluded; the church reads to us from the gospels for us to consider, weigh and imitate. But because she knows that our own thinking can never lead to the heart of God, that our prayer lacks wings to take it up unless it is carried by God's Spirit, she plunges all the moral meanings into this Spirit.

Christ comes to us in two ways which are really only one. There is a Christ of history and a Christ of faith; but the two are one: it would be dangerous to regard only the one or the other. Jesus, a man living in time, could not redeem us, the Christ we see in the mysteries alone would move in a breathless air. Our redemption rests upon the fact that God has really appeared in the flesh and that this man is the Son of God and *Kyrios*, glorified at the Father's right hand. He became *Kyrios, pneuma*. He is the same Lord who walked unnoticed and persecuted through the fields of Palestine, ending his life like a criminal on the cross; now he rules the world as King and the church is his bride. All his life, beginning in the Virgin's womb, is the great mystery of salvation, hidden from eternity in God and now revealed in the *ecclesia*.

From *The Mystery of Christian Worship,* 1962, Darton, Longman & Todd. Used by kind permission of the publisher.

Friday of the first week of Advent

The Presence of the Lord
Adrian Nocent

The special nature of the liturgical year is that the Lord himself presides over it and that he celebrates his mysteries with the church for the glory of the Father. The highest form of his presence is the real presence in the Eucharist, and it is the source and summit of all liturgical celebration because it is the presence of the paschal mystery. On the other hand, each Eucharistic celebration, while having the paschal mystery as its basis and background, derives its particular features and colouring from the celebration of the liturgy of the word. The Eucharistic celebration on Christmas is different from, as well as the same as, the Eucharistic celebration of the day when the Pentecostal Spirit was sent. The celebration of the word gives each Eucharistic celebration its special colouring.

The Bible, by itself a dead book, becomes alive and actual when it is proclaimed in the liturgical assembly. There is more than one 'real' presence and we must not exclude all presences but the Eucharistic one. Pope Paul VI writes that 'this presence of Christ in the Eucharist is called "real" not to exclude the idea that others are "real" too, but rather to indicate presence *par excellence.*' According to Pope Paul VI, there are several modes of real presence. What distinguishes them is not the realness of the presence but the mode of it; this diversifies them and gives them each its own 'level'.

The important thing is that the presence of the Lord in the proclamation of the Word is not analogical and figurative, as when someone reads the work of a poet and entitles the reading: 'The Abiding Presence of ...' In the proclamation of the Word there is a real, active presence of the Lord. This notion is still unfamiliar and has not become part of the instinctive habits of mind of our contemporaries, whose attention is still focused exclusively on the real Eucharistic presence.

From *The Liturgical Year: Advent, Christmas, Epiphany,* Collegeville, MN: The Liturgical Press, 1977. Used by kind permission of the publisher.

Saturday of the first week of Advent

To Believe
Karl Barth

Zechariah was mute because he did not believe the angel. We are like Zechariah in the sanctuary. 'Gabriel who stands before God,' spoke to him. This angel stands before God, but sometimes, in the sanctuary, he also stands before us. He speaks with God, but he also speaks with us.

The living word of God is available to us. It is a word that, in contrast to all human words, is clear, intelligible and unambiguous. Yes, this inward word of God, which God speaks to us by means of his angels, contains precisely that which so moves and unsettles us.

God spoke to Zechariah of something quite grand – a coming great decision and turning of all things, of the approaching better age at hand, of the Saviour, and of his herald, whose father he himself would become.

Even if we have never seen angels standing 'on the right of the incense altar,' the fire of God can actually burn us, the earthquake of God can shake us, God's flood can rush around us, his storm can seize us.

Believing is not something as special and difficult or even unnatural as we often suppose. Believing means that what we listen to, we listen to as God's speech. What moves us is not just our own concern, but God's concern.

So now here we stand, simultaneously deaf and mute like Zechariah. In spite of his unbelief, he was still a herald of Advent, one who waited for God. Otherwise the angel would not have spoken to him. Nor would he have become the father of John the Baptist. When everything came to pass which he could not believe and could not express, then he was suddenly able to believe and to speak. For God does not stand still whenever we come to a standstill, but precedes us with his deeds and only waits so that we can follow. And so we will accept – even with all that we cannot say, and with all that we have not yet heard – that we are also heralds of Advent. We will finally believe, and then we will also hear.

From 'Lucas 1:5-23' in *Predigten*, 1917, pp 423-431, Theologischer Verlag, Zürich, 1999, trs Robert J. Sherman in *Watch for the Light: Readings for Advent and Christmas*, Orbis Books, Maryknoll, New York, 2004.

Second Sunday of Advent

Christ's saving deeds in time
Odo Casel

The mystery reveals to us the real meaning of Christ's saving deeds in time. It takes none of the concreteness from them, but places them in their real, divine context, showing them to be part of God's saving plan, hidden from eternity revealed now in time, and flowing back into eternity.

When the church year celebrates historical occurrences and developments, it does not do so for their own sake but for the eternity hidden within them. The great deed of God, the redeeming work of Christ, is its content. This content is not a gradual unfolding in the way a calendar year unfolds and develops: there is a single divine act which demands and finds gradual accustoming on our part, though in itself it is complete. When the church year fashions and forms a kind of unfolding of the mystery of Christ, it does not seek to provide historical drama, it seeks to help us step by step to approach God, an approach which was first made to us through God's own revelation of himself. It is the entire saving mystery which is before the eyes of the church and each one of us, more concretely on each occasion.

We celebrate Advent, not by putting ourselves back into the state of unredeemed humankind, but in the certainty of the Lord who has already appeared to us, for whom we must prepare ourselves; the longing of ancient piety is our model and our master. We do not celebrate Lent as if we had never been redeemed, but as having the stamp of the

cross upon us, and now only seeking to be better conformed to the death of Christ, so that the resurrection may
be always more clearly shown upon us.

From *The Mystery of Christian Worship*, 1962, Darton, Longman &
Todd. Used by kind permission of the publisher.

Monday of the second week of Advent

Today, if you should hear his voice
Odo Casel

The church, although always possessing the whole mystery of Christ, can still, on certain days when a definite aspect of it is brought into light, sing 'today': at Christmas, 'today Christ is born'; Epiphany, 'today the heavenly bridegroom is joined to the church'; Easter, 'this is the day which the Lord has made'; Pentecost, 'today the Spirit descended upon the disciples in tongues of fire.' The entire holy year is an image of the eternal design of God. As the year is an image of the life of each one of us, each day too, with its rising of light and life, its growth to zenith and descent to sleep, forms an image which can serve as framework and symbol of the mystery of Christ. As Christ's sacrificial death is the climax of the world's history, Mass is the climax of each day. All about this climax, in smaller and greater circles group the other prayers, like smaller peaks on the slopes of the highest one. The whole day office of the church is the gold setting for the jewel of this sacrifice.

There are paintings which present simply landscape and atmosphere with such intensity that some tiny figures are required to give the moving eyes a place of rest. In others the action depicted so dominates the whole that the background seems to have no weight at all. Still other works have figures and background completely in harmony; the surroundings put the figures into a proper frame, whereas the figures give the whole composition greater depth: the line which starts with the figures continues in the trees, the buildings and the other natural features. Undoubtedly this last is a good solution to the artistic problem, and the church has constructed the Mass and the Office on a similar plan. The mystery which is hidden and silent within the sacrificial action, and which the canon seeks to express, continues in the office and is, so to speak, resolved into the colours of the spectrum. Much that could only be hinted at in the centre shows itself in various places and is submitted to loving contemplation. The mysteries of God's saving design and grace are all depicted and presented in daily prayers, which find their crown and fulfilment in the sacramental mystery of the altar; all the rich and varied lines converge upon the sacrifice and broken colours revert to a shining unity.

So the office moves about a firm pole, the presence and display in ritual of the great event which is at the heart of the Christian mystery: redemption through incarnation, death and resurrection. All the church's prayer and all our prayer become the prayer of Christ. Christ's Spirit, the Holy Spirit, carries up our prayer on strong wings and gives it a divine worth it could never have of itself.

From *The Mystery of Christian Worship,* 1962, Darton, Longman & Todd. Used by kind permission of the publisher.

Tuesday of second week of Advent

The whole church year is a single mystery
Odo Casel

The whole church year is a single mystery. Its high point is
mystery in the highest sense, the *sacramentum paschale*, the
sacrificial mystery which is brought to us again each
Sunday.

Out of the paschal mystery, which in the first age of
liturgy was the one ruling motif, there developed the
epiphany, for which Advent (the word *Adventus* comes from
the Greek *epiphaneia*) prepares us even today, although the
Christmas feast has now been placed before it. The showing,
epiphany, includes Christmas but is more than the feast of
Christ's birth. Again, it is the entire redemptive mystery,
seen under the viewpoint of the incarnation. When God
takes flesh, he consecrates it. Is there, then, a proper mystery
of the incarnation, as there is of Christ's death? No. We
celebrate the culmination of epiphany, too, by the memorial
of Christ's death: redemption was first finished upon the
cross. Epiphany is, therefore, the entire mystery of redemption,
seen from another vantage point.

The mystery of the church's year is one. Does this
emphasis on unity take away from the attractiveness of
variety? No; unity does not mean uniformity. The more
single an idea, the deeper it is and the more powerfully it
fills the mind: so its fullness seeks an outlet in a variety of
rites. The Mass is always the high-point of liturgy. But from
the source a mighty stream of mysteries flows into the
church's ground, and on its banks the Spirit's Word forms

ever new pictures in the liturgy, to clothe and express the rites.

> For just as from the heavens the rain and snow come down And do not return there till they have watered the earth, making it fertile and fruitful,
>
> Giving seed to him who sows and bread to him who eats,
>
> So shall my word be that goes forth from my mouth; It shall not return to me void, but shall do my will, achieving the end for which I sent it. (Isaiah 55:10-11)

From *The Mystery of Christian Worship,* 1962, Darton, Longman & Todd. Used by kind permission of the publisher.

Wednesday of the second week of Advent

The Benedictus
Raymond E. Brown

One may call the Benedictus a christological hymn since it concerns the Messiah, 'the horn of salvation' which, as in Hannah's canticle (in 1 Samuel 2:10) refers to the Messiah, Christ, as 'the horn of his anointed.'

Yet it is very different from the christological hymns we find in the Pauline and Johannine traditions, which spell out the human career of Jesus. For instance, the hymn that Paul quotes in Philippians (2:6-11) speaks of Jesus' origins, his humble life as a servant, his obedient death on the cross, and his exaltation. The Johannine Prologue hymn (John 1:1-18) speaks of his coming into the world, being rejected by his own, and manifesting his glory. The Benedictus, however, describes the messianic salvation entirely in Old Testament terms without appealing to any event in Jesus' life. One cannot explain that phenomenon simply from the fact that, in the narrative context in which Luke has placed the canticle, none of the events of Jesus' life had yet taken place, for Luke did not hesitate to insert references to what the Baptist would do. Rather, in the Benedictus and in the other Lucan canticles, we are hearing very early Christian christology that did not require and perhaps had not yet acquired a peculiarly Christian vocabulary – perhaps the oldest preserved Christian prayers of praise wherein Jewish believers expressed themselves entirely in the language of their ancestors.

Such an insight shows how appropriate is the use of the

Benedictus as an Advent hymn. This is the season where we relive the story of Israel and its expectations; we who believe that that story is encapsulated in Jesus and those expectations are fulfilled in him, praise God in the language of Israel whenever we recite the Benedictus.

From *A Coming Christ in Advent,* Collegeville, MN: The Liturgical Press, 1988. Used by kind permission of the publisher.

Thursday of the second week of Advent

John the Baptist
Patrick Fitzgerald-Lombard

All four gospels put a stress on John the Baptist fulfilling
the prophecy from Isaiah and this may have been John's
own assessment of his mission. He is linked with the
expected messenger of the prophet Elijah; this may come
from Jesus himself (Mt 17:10-13). As the church grew it
claimed John the Baptist as its own. Many Christians probably
came to Jesus through John (Jn 1:37). So the gospels show
John as a model Christian. The church has always seen in
John a means of setting out its own part in the preparation
of the way of the Lord. John the Baptist is an image of the
church as a herald, proclaiming the good news of Jesus to
the world.

The Benedictus shows us the foundation for being
heralds of the Lord. Our hope for the future, the good
news which we proclaim, receives its conviction because we
know that God has fulfilled his promises in the past. Our
Advent liturgy reminds us that the yearning of Judaism for
the Day of the Lord has already happened in Jesus Christ.
We still yearn for the second coming of the Lord in glory.
Advent allows us to pray for greater strength as we prepare
for the Second Advent.

This is the setting for John the Baptist, the prophet. As a
prophet John was courageously able to speak the word of
God to the people of his generation. He was not part of
the system of government (Mt 11:8). On the contrary, he
kept independent of it and was prepared to denounce its

excesses. This resulted in his arrest and execution. John the Baptist calls us to work for social justice in our world today. We have to be prepared to stand back from human institutions. We have to be prepared to suffer. For this, we must go into the wilderness in order to see clearly the message, the values of the good news.

Even so, what will happen will be unexpected. John had to change his attitudes because the Messiah who came was not what he anticipated (Mt 11:2). Our preparation for the Second Advent requires the ability to listen and to be open. In many languages 'obedience' and 'hearing' are similar words. To hear is to obey. We talk about obeying the will of God, yet it is all too easy to settle down and become fixed in our ways. The word of God will always challenge us because it will be fulfilled in ways that we do not expect.

John the Baptist was the herald of the final age. His birth and his ministry came with joy and with the outpouring of the Holy Spirit. We have received the baptism of the Holy Spirit (Mk 1:8) given to us by the risen Lord. This makes us more than prophets, we become witnesses to Christ. Our mission as heralds is to point to Christ, to make him known when he comes. We are lamps reflecting the light of Christ. In this way the church becomes a beacon of hope for the world.

From *Scripture in Church*, issue 36, Dominican Publications, Dublin. Used by kind permission of the publishers.

Friday of the second week of Advent

Watching for Christ
John Henry Newman

What it is to *watch* for Christ? He says, '*Watch* ye therefore, for ye know not when the Master of the house cometh; at evening, or at midnight, or at the cock-crowing, or in the morning; lest coming suddenly he find you sleeping. And what I say unto you, I say unto all, *Watch*.' In like manner he upbraided Peter thus: 'Simon, sleepest thou? couldest not thou *watch* one hour?' (Mark 14:37). In like manner St Paul in his Epistle to the Romans: 'Now it is high time to awake out of sleep ... The night is far spent, the day is at hand' (Rom 13:11, 12).

Now I consider this word *watching*, first used by our Lord, then by the favoured disciple, then by the two great apostles, Peter and Paul, is a remarkable word, remarkable because the idea is not so obvious as might appear at first sight, and next because they all inculcate it. We are not simply to believe, but to *watch*; not simply to love, but to *watch*; not simply to obey, but to *watch*; to *watch* for what? for that great event, Christ's coming. Whether then we consider what is the obvious meaning of the word, or the Object towards which it directs us, we seem to see a special duty enjoined on us, such as does not naturally come into our minds. Most of us have a general idea what is meant by believing, fearing, loving, and obeying; but perhaps we do not contemplate or apprehend what is meant by *watching*.

Do you know the feeling in matters of this life, of expecting a friend, expecting him to come, and he delays?

Do you know what it is to be in unpleasant company, and to wish for the time to pass away, and the hour strike when you may be at liberty? Do you know what it is to be in anxiety lest something should happen which may happen or may not, or to be in suspense about some important event, which makes your heart beat when you are reminded of it, and of which you think the first thing in the morning? Do you know what it is to have a friend in a distant country, to expect news of him, and to wonder from day to day what he is now doing, and whether he is well? Do you know what it is so to live upon a person who is present with you, that your eyes follow his, that you read his soul, that you see all its changes in his countenance, that you anticipate his wishes, that you smile in his smile, and are sad in his sadness, and are downcast when he is vexed, and rejoice in his successes? To *watch* for Christ is a feeling such as all these; as far as feelings of this world are fit to shadow out those of another.

He watches for Christ who has a sensitive, eager, apprehensive mind; who is awake, alive, quick-sighted, zealous in seeking and honouring him; who looks out for him in all that happens, and who would not be surprised, who would not be over-agitated or overwhelmed, if he found that he was coming at once.

From *Parochial and Plain Sermons*, vol 4.

Saturday of the second week of Advent

The Tender Time of Advent
Caryll Houselander

When a woman is carrying a child she develops a certain instinct of self-defence. It is not selfishness; it is not egoism. It is an absorption into the life within, a folding of self like a little tent around the child's frailty, a God-like instinct to cherish, and some day to bring forth, the life. A closing upon it like the petals of a flower closing upon the dew that shines in its heart. This is precisely the attitude we must have to Christ, the life within us, in the Advent of our contemplation.

By his own will Christ was dependent on Mary during Advent: he was absolutely helpless; he could go nowhere but where she chose to take him; he could not speak; her breathing was his breath; his heart beat in the beating of her heart. Today Christ is dependent upon us.

This dependence of Christ lays a great trust upon us. During this tender time of Advent we must carry him in our hearts to wherever he wants to go, and there are many places to which he may never go unless we take him to them.

Excerpted from *The Reed of God* by Caryll Houselander, (c) 2006. Used with permission from the publisher, Christian Classics, PO Box 428, Notre Dame, Indiana 46556, www.avemariapress.com.

Third Sunday of Advent

Gaudete
Karl Rahner

As the autumn season fades and winter takes over, the world becomes still. Everything around us turns pale and drab. It chills us. We are least inclined to hectic activities. More than in other seasons of the year, we prefer to stay at home and be alone. It is as if the world had become subdued and had lost the courage to assert its self-satisfaction, the courage to be proud of its power and its life. Its progressive growth in the swelling fullness of the spring and summer has failed, for the fullness has vanished. In this season, time itself bears eloquent witness to its own poverty. It disappoints us.

Here is the moment to conquer the melancholy of time, here is the moment to say softly and sincerely what we know by faith: '*Gaudete*, let us rejoice. I believe in the eternity of God who has entered into our time, my time. Beneath the wearisome coming and going of chronological time, life that no longer knows death is already secretly growing. It is already here, it is already in me, precisely because I believe.'

Time is no longer the bleak, empty, fading succession of moments, one moment destroying the preceding one and causing it to become 'past,' only to die away itself, clearing the way for the future that presses – itself already mortally wounded. Time itself is redeemed. It possesses a centre that can preserve the present and gather into itself the future, a nucleus that fills the present with a future that is already effected, a focal point that co-ordinates the living present with the eternal future. The advent of the incarnate God, of the Christ who is the same yesterday and today and in eternity – this advent has penetrated into this time that is to be redeemed.

A 'now' of eternity is in you. And this 'now' has already begun to gather together your earthly moments into itself. For into your heart comes the One who is himself Advent, the Boundless Future who is already in the process of coming, the Lord himself, who has already come into the time of the flesh to redeem it.

From *The Eternal Year*, Burns & Oates, London, 1964. Used by kind permission of Continuum International Publishing Group Ltd.

Monday of the third week of Advent

'This is Meister Eckhart from whom God hid nothing'
A Christmas sermon of Meister Eckhart

'*Dum Medium Silentium*, while all things were wrapped in silence and night was in the midst of its swift course …' Because the same One, who is begotten and born of God the Father, without ceasing in eternity, is born today, within time, in human nature, we make a holiday to celebrate it. St Augustine says that this birth is always happening. And yet, if it does not happen in me, what use is it? Everything depends on this.

'Out of the silence, a secret word was spoken to me.' What is that silence and where is that word to be spoken? The central silence is the purest element of the soul, the soul's most exalted place, the core, where no creature may enter, nor any idea, and there the soul neither thinks nor acts, nor entertains any idea, either of itself or of anything else.

What should we do to secure and deserve the occurrence and perfection of this birth in us? Should we co-operate by imagining and thinking about God, or should we keep quiet, be silent and at peace, so that God may speak and act through us? Should we do nothing but wait until God does act?

I repeat, as I have said before, that the best life and the loftiest is to be silent and to let God speak and act through us. The prophet has said: 'I will sit and be silent and listen to what God shall say in me.'

'In the middle of the night, while all things were wrapped in silence, a secret word was spoken to me.' It came stealthily, like a thief. It opened and shone before me as if it were revealing something and made me conscious of

God, and so it was called 'a word'. Furthermore it was not clear to me what it was, because it came with stealth like a whisper trying to explain itself through the stillness.

St Paul says that we are to hunt it and track it down and never give up until we get it. Once he was caught up into the third heaven of the knowledge of God and saw everything. When he came back, he had forgotten nothing but it had so regressed into the core of his soul that he could not call it up to mind. It was covered up. He had to pursue it within and not without. It is always within and never outside – but always inward.

St Augustine has something to say about this: 'I am aware of something in myself, like a light dancing before my soul, and if it could be brought out with perfect steadiness, it would surely be life eternal. It hides, and then again, it shows. It comes like a thief, as if it would steal everything from the soul. But since it shows itself and draws attention, it must want to allure the soul and make the soul follow it, to rob the soul of self.'

Taste now the profit and fruit of this secret word and this darkness. Not only the Son of the heavenly Father is born in the darkness which is his own, but you, too, are born there, a child of the same heavenly Father, and to you also he gives power.

May God, newly born in human form, eternally help us, that we frail people, being born in him, may be divine.

From *Meister Eckhart, a modern translation,* by Raymond Bernard Blakney, Harper & Row, New York, 1941. Used by kind permission of HarperCollins, New York.

Tuesday of the third week of Advent

Eckhart's Teaching
David Appelbaum

Meister Eckhart belongs to an ancient and secret tradition
that concerns the secret birth of awakened consciousness.
Awakening is the 'fire' mentioned by Jesus when he counsels
Nicodemus on the inner path in the third chapter of John's
gospel. It is this path that Eckhart walks, a path that wakens
consciousness to the meaning of awakening, symbolised in
its initial state by water and by the ritual of baptismal
immersion. This is also part of what Jesus communicates to
Nicodemus during the latter's dark night. But just as a
creature of water does not know the element it lives in, so
too is consciousness unaware of its inborn wakeful state.
The discernment of wakefulness and its call is the birthing
of an awakened vision.

   This particular teaching of Jesus, the path of awakening
consciousness, is emphasised by Maximus the Confessor,
who says, 'By grace which calls, Christ comes incessantly to
be engendered mystically in the soul, by taking on flesh
through those who receive salvation: thus he makes the
soul, by which he is brought forth, a mother, while allowing
its virginity to remain intact.' Dionysius the Areopagite calls
this path 'an initiation into theogenesis'. Theogenesis, the
birth of God, is the advent of Christ-awareness, an awakened
state in which the most fundamental dualism is shattered,
that between God and his creature. Theogenesis is the final
fruit of the annunciation. It is to this ancient path, newly
rediscovered and uttered afresh by Jesus, that Eckhart invites

us, his readers 655 years later, to follow. Eckhart's single-pointed concern is with the mystery of birth. As Jesus said to Nicodemus, there is a second birth: 'Ye must be born *anothen.*' Although *anothen* is usually translated as 'again' (as in 'ye must be born again'), in the Greek it also means 'from above'. The thorough penetration of our daily mind by a higher consciousness enables us to slough off our entrancement by things that don't matter. The hidden teaching of God's birth in a human being requires the utmost rigour to uncover. It depends on emptying me of me, and so necessarily takes place in the desert. *Metanoia*, the repentance which is also a radical 'change of mind', requires being in the wilderness, where the God beyond God alone dwells. Only when that final dualism is shattered does a human being fulfil his or her destiny. Human destiny lies in becoming empty, for emptiness is the womb in which the word-seed becomes the Word, and the Only Son is thereby born. God loves nothing better than the desert, where the seeker goes to give birth to God and participate in the joy of birth. There he himself must bring to an end the dualism between creature and Creator and be born in humankind. By that act, God becomes nothing, as empty as the desert, and, dissolved, only the God beyond God remains.

From *Wandering Joy, Meister Eckhart's Mystical Philosophy, Translations and Commentary* by Reiner Schürmann, Introduction by David Appelbaum, Lindisfarne Books, USA, 2001. Used by kind permission of the publisher.

Wednesday of the third week of Advent

A Giving
Brendan Kennelly

Here in this room, this December day,
Listening to the year die on the warfields
And in the voices of children
Who laugh in the indecisive light
At the throes that but rehearse their own
I take the mystery of giving in my hands
And pass it on to you.

I give thanks
To the giver of images,
The reticent God who goes about his work
Determined to hold on to nothing.
Embarrassed at the prospect of possession
He distributes leaves to the wind
And lets them pitch and leap like boys capering out of their skin.
Pictures are thrown behind hedges,
Poems skitter backwards over cliffs,
There is a loaf of bread on Derek's threshold
And we will never know who put it there.

For such things
And bearing in mind
The midnight hurt, the shot bride,
The famine in the heart,
The demented soldier, the terrified cities
Rising out of their own rubble,

I give thanks.
I listen to the sound of doors
Opening and closing in the street.
They are like the heartbeats of this creator
Who gives everything away.

I do not understand
Such constant evacuation of the heart,
Such striving towards emptiness,

Thinking, however, of the intrepid skeleton,
The feared definition,
I grasp a little of the giving
And hold it close as my own flesh.

It is this little
That I give to you.
And now I want to walk out and witness
The shadow of some ungraspable sweetness
Passing over the measureless squalor of man
Like a child's hand over my own face
Or the exodus of swallows across the land

And I know it does not matter
That I do not understand.

From *Familiar Strangers: New and Selected Poems 1960-2004*,
Bloodaxe Books, 2004. Used by kind permission of the publisher.

Thursday of the third week of Advent

Newgrange of the Heart
John O'Donohue

It is always astonishing how love can strike. No context is love-proof, no convention or commitment impervious. Even a lifestyle which is perfectly insulated, where the personality is controlled, all the days ordered and all actions in sequence, can to its own dismay find that an unexpected spark has landed; it begins to smoulder until it is finally unquenchable. The force of Eros always brings disturbance; in the concealed terrain of the human heart Eros remains a light sleeper.

Creation is imbued with Eros. Each landscape, each season has its own quiet Eros. In contrast to the glory of autumnal colour which is like the flaming of a final twilight, winter is a chaste season. Nothing flourishes. Every field and tree is cleaned back to its bare form. The night of winter comes in clear and sure. Against the bleak grey whatever muted colour endures seems ghost-like. But as ever, the circle travels on to its own beginning. And just when the amnesia seems absolute, the first tones of spring commence their infant flaming. Within a short while the exiled Eros of nature stages a magnificent return. From the dark underlife of cold fields, infinite tribes of grass ascend. Skeleton trees allow themselves a shimmering of leaves. Flowers arrive as if this were the place they had always dreamed. The terse silence of winter gives way to the symphony of spring. Eros has awakened. Birth is the inner and outer song of spring. If winter is the oldest season, then spring is the youngest season. The Eros of the earth calls forth the beauty of spring.

Eros is a divine force. It infuses all the earth. Without it, the earth would be a bare, cold planet for Eros is the soul of the earth. In the embrace of Eros the earth becomes a *terra illuminata*. Amidst the vast expanse of fields and seas, the providence of Eros awakens and sustains the longing of the earth.

From *Divine Beauty,* by John O'Donohue, published by Bantam Press. Reprinted by permission of the Random House Group Ltd.

Friday of the third week of Advent

The Dangers of Advent
J. B. Phillips

The particular danger which faces us as Christmas
approaches is unlikely to be contempt for the sacred season,
but nevertheless our familiarity with it may easily produce
in us a kind of indifference. The true wonder and mystery
may leave us unmoved; familiarity may easily blind us to
the shining fact that lies at the heart of Christmastide.

  What we are in fact celebrating is the awe-inspiring
humility of God, and no amount of familiarity with the
trappings of Christmas should ever blind us to its quiet but
explosive significance. For Christians believe that so great is
God's love and concern for humanity that he himself
became a man. Amid the sparkle and colour and music of
the day's celebration we do well to remember that God's
insertion of himself into human history was achieved with
an almost frightening quietness and humility.

  This almost beggarly beginning has been romanticised
by artists and poets throughout the centuries. Yet I believe
that at least once a year we should look steadily at the historic
fact, and not at any pretty picture. At the time of this
astonishing event only a handful of people knew what had
happened. And as far as we know, no one spoke openly
about it for thirty years. Even when the baby was grown to
be a man, only a few recognised him for who he really was.
Two or three years of teaching and preaching and healing
people, and his work was finished. He was betrayed and
judicially murdered, deserted at the end by all his friends.

By normal human standards this is a tragic little tale of failure, the rather squalid story of a promising young man from a humble home, put to death by the envy and malice of the professional men of religion. All this happened in an obscure, occupied province of the vast Roman Empire.

It is two thousand years ago that this apparently invincible Empire utterly collapsed, and all that is left of it is ruins. Yet the baby, born in such pitiful humility and cut down as a young man in his prime, commands the allegiance of millions of people all over the world. Although they have never seen him, he has become friend and companion to innumerable people. This undeniable fact is, by any measurement, the most astonishing phenomenon in human history. It is a solid rock of evidence that no agnostic can ever explain away.

From 'The Christian Year' from *Good News: Thoughts on God and Man*, The Macmillan Co, New York, 1963.

Saturday of the third week of Advent

The Disarming Child
Jürgen Moltmann

Anyone who belongs to the people who dwell in the land of darkness, or anyone who has ever belonged to it, will find this message about the disarming birth of the child as alluring as it is unbelievable. The people in deep darkness: Whom does this mean?

In the prophet's time it was that section of Israel that had fallen under Assyrian dictatorship. Every imprisoned Israelite knew the tramp of the invading boots, the bloody coats and the rods of the slave-drivers. Today we can still see Assyrian warriors and overseers like this in the frescoes, with their iron shoes, their cloaks and their sticks. But for the prophet, Assyria is more than just Assyria. She is the representative of the power that is hostile to God, and this makes her at the same time the very quintessence of all inhuman oppression. The prophet looks at the specific plight of his people, but talks about a misery experienced by people everywhere. That is why his words and images are so wide open that prisoners in every age have been able to find in them their own fate and their own hope.

A people in darkness: let me add a personal word. This phrase touched me directly when in 1945 we were driven in endless and desolate columns into the prisoner-of-war camps, the sticks of the guards at our sides, with hungry stomachs and empty hearts and curses on our lips. But many of us then, and I was one, glimpsed the light that radiates from the divine child. This light did not allow me to perish. This hope kept us alive.

A people in darkness: today I see before me the millions of the imprisoned, the exiled, the deported, the tortured and the silenced everywhere in the world where people are pushed into this darkness.

This divided world is increasingly capable of turning into a universal prison camp. And we are faced with the burning question: on which side of the barbed wire are we living, and at whose cost? The people in darkness sees the great light. To this people – to them first of all – the light shines in all its brightness. To these people the child is born, for the peace of us all.

From *The Power of the Powerless*, SCM Press, London, 1983. Used by kind permission of the publishers.

Fourth Sunday of Advent

As Christmas approaches
Vincent Ryan

The word Advent designated originally not the period of preparation, but the feast of Christmas itself. The coming of Christ in the flesh and the liturgical commemoration of that event was the *adventus Domini*, the advent of the Lord. And since in the New Testament the word *Adventus* translated the Greek *Parousia*, it was natural that the term should include reference to the second coming of Christ at the end of time. Advent was a late development in Rome. The Roman Church did not see the need for a prolonged pre-Christmas fast. This notion came from Spain and Gaul.

The time of immediate preparation for Christmas can be dated from 17 December. Why? Because, before the Roman Advent was organised in the sixth century, the churches of Christian Gaul and Spain began their preparation for Christmas and Epiphany on this date. It was just three weeks before the Epiphany, a feast of very great importance for these churches, and a day on which baptism was conferred.

As to its essential form and structure, the development of the Roman Advent was completed by the eighth century. It was profoundly influenced by the penitential spirit of the older Gallican Advent, but it still managed to retain its own message of joyful hope. Among the more splendid additions to this Roman Advent liturgy must be included the O Antiphons or Greater Antiphons. These have been in use in our western liturgy since the time of Charlemagne.

Amalarius of Metz attributes their composition to an anonymous cantor who probably lived in the eighth century.

As Christmas approaches, the church seems to count the days as we ourselves counted the days to the holidays when we were at school. We arrive at Christmas eve. The liturgy appropriates passages from the Old Testament to express the imminence of Christ's coming. 'Know today that the Lord will come; in the morning you will see his glory.' This comes from the Book of Exodus and, in its original context, refers to the miraculous feeding of the Israelites in the desert. Such texts place us in the context of salvation history. The imagery of the passover and the exodus throw light on the mystery we are about to celebrate. 'Lift up your heads for your redemption is at hand;' 'Tomorrow your salvation will be with you, says the Lord God Almighty;' 'Tomorrow is the day on which the sins of the world will be wiped away. The Saviour of the world will rule us himself.'

From *Advent to Epiphany,* Veritas Publications 1982. Used by kind permission of the publisher.

Monday of the fourth week of Advent

The Birth of God in me
A Christmas sermon of Meister Eckhart

The greatest good that God ever performed for us was that he became a human being. I ought to tell a story that is very apposite here.

There were a rich husband and wife. The wife suffered a misfortune through which she lost an eye, and she was much distressed by this. Then her husband came to her and said: 'Madam, why are you so distressed? You should not distress yourself so because you have lost an eye.' Then she said: 'Sir, I am not distressing myself about the fact that I have lost my eye; what distresses me is that it seems to me that you will love me less because of it.' Then he said: 'Madam, I do love you.' Not long after that he gouged out one of his own eyes and came to his wife and said: 'Madam, to make you believe that I love you, I have made myself like you; now I too have only one eye.'

This stands for us, who could scarcely believe that God loved us so much, until God gouged out one of his own eyes and took upon himself human nature. This is what 'being made flesh' is. Our Lady said: 'How should this happen?' Then the angel said: 'The Holy Spirit will come down from above into you,' from the highest throne, from the Father of eternal light.

'A Child is born to us, a son is given to us,' a child in the smallness of its human nature, a Son in its everlasting divinity. The authorities say: 'All created things behave as they do because they want to give birth and they want to resemble the Father.' God acts like that: He gives birth to his Only-Begotten Son. And as he gives birth to his Only-Begotten Son into me, so I give him birth again into the Father.

Tuesday of the fourth week of Advent

The Disarming Child
Jürgen Moltmann

All the images the prophet uses to paint the possible future point to one fact: the birth of the divine child. The burning of the weapons, the jubilation and the great lights are all caught up in the birth of God's peace-bringer. They are all to be found in him. Now the prophet stops talking in intoxicating images and thrilling comparisons, and comes to the heart of the matter: the person of the divine liberator: 'To us a child is born. To us a son is given.' This future is wholly and entirely God's initiative. That is why it is so totally different from our human plans and possibilities. If liberation and peace are bound up with the birth of a little helpless and defenceless child, then their future lies in the hands of God alone. On the human side, all we can see here is weakness and helplessness. It is not the pride and strength of the grown man which are proclaimed on the threshhold of the kingdom, but the defencelessness and the hope of the child.

Emperors have always liked to be called emperors of peace, from Augustus down to the present day. Their opponents and the heroes of the people have always liked to be called 'liberators,' from the Cherusci to Simón Bolívar. They have come and gone. Neither their rule nor their liberation endured. God was not with them. Their zeal was not the zeal of the Lord. They did not disarm this divided world. They could not forgive the guilt, because they themselves were not innocent. Their hope did not bring new life. So let them go their way. Let us deny them our complete obedience. 'To us this child is born.' The divine liberty lies on his shoulders.

There is nothing against dreams if they are good ones. The prophet gave the people in darkness, and us, this unforgettable dream. We should remain true to it.

From *The Power of the Powerless*, SCM Press, London, 1983. Used by kind permission of the publishers.

Wednesday of the fourth week of Advent

A place in my heart for You
Gertrude the Great of Helfta

One day I entered the courtyard, sat down by the fishpond and was overcome by the beauty of these surroundings. The limpidity of the flowing water, the green of the trees, the flight of the birds, the doves in particular, but above all the secret peacefulness of it all. I began to wonder what could be added to this place to make its joy complete.

I must have a friend, I thought, a devoted and familiar friend, to assuage my loneliness. You, my God, drew my thoughts to you. Certainly it was you who inspired me. You showed me that my heart could be a dwelling-place for you. Like this flowing water, I must be thankful for what you have suggested to me and direct the flow of my thoughts back to you. Like these trees, flourishing in the goodness of green, I must increase in strength and devote myself to good works. Like these doves flying, I must seek the things of heaven. In this way, my heart will provide you with a dwelling comparable to the delights of this place.

The whole day long my mind was full of this idea. In the evening before I went to bed, as I knelt to pray, I thought of the words of Scripture: 'If someone loves me, they will keep my word, and my Father will love them, and we will come and make our home with them.' Then I felt in my heart that you had come.

From *Gertrude d'Helfta: Oeuvres spirituelles II:* Le Héraut (Livre II, chapitre 3) Paris, Editions du Cerf, 1968.

Thursday of the fourth week of Advent

God's Birth in Us
Ladislaus Boros

I would like to consider. We can think of the three traditional
Masses on Christmas day as representing the threefold birth
of Christ: his birth in the Trinity, his birth in history and his
birth in us. Christ's birth in the Trinity is celebrated at midnight and the Mass begins with the words: 'The Lord said
to me: "You are my son, today I have begotten you".' God,
revelation tells us, is three in one. God is eternally coming
into being, eternally as the witness, the Father, eternally
proceeding, as the Son, and eternally as circling love, the
Holy Spirit.

The second Mass opens with the words: 'Today a light
will shine upon us.' The son of God became man one night
two thousand years ago in a village called Bethlehem. This
is the great mystery of Christmas.

The third Mass begins: 'For to us a child is born; to us a
son is given.' This symbolises the birth that takes place every
day in each one of us. Being a Christian means growing
together with Christ. In the words of the Fathers of the
church: 'God became man so that we might become God.'
The essence of God's becoming man was his emptying of
himself. Every Christian is bound at some time or other to
empty themselves. We realise this attitude of Jesus in our
lives by leaving ourselves behind in selfless love and service
of others. In heaven, what began in the Trinity, continued at
Bethlehem and has been realised throughout the history of
Christian life will be fully revealed.

In this way, Jesus prepares for his second and last coming in glory. This last Christmas in the world will continue in eternity. It is known as heaven.

From *Meditations*, Search Press, 1973. Used by kind permission of Continuum International Publishing Group.

Friday of the fourth week of Advent

The Dangers of Advent
J. B. Phillips

By far the most important and significant event in the whole course of human history will be celebrated, with or without understanding, at the end of this season, Advent. The towering miracle of God's visit to this planet on which we live will be glossed over, brushed aside or rendered impotent by over-familiarity. Even by the believer, the full weight of the event is not always appreciated. Our faith is in Jesus Christ – we believe with all our hearts that this man, who lived and died and rose again in Palestine, was truly the Son of God. We may have, in addition, some working experience that the man Jesus is still alive, and yet be largely unaware of the intense meaning of what we believe.

As a translator of the New Testament I find in it no support whatever for the belief that one day all evil will be eradicated from the earth, all problems solved, and health and wealth be everyone's portion! Even among some Christians such a belief is quite commonly held, so that the 'second advent' of Christ is no more and no less than the infinite number of 'comings' of Christ into our minds.

In my judgement, the description which Christ gave of the days that were to come before his return is more accurately reproduced in this fear-ridden age than ever before in human history. Of course we do not know the times and the seasons, but at least we can refuse to be deceived by the current obsession for physical security in the here-and-now.

While we continue to pray and work for the spread of the kingdom in this transitory world, we know that its centre of gravity is not here at all. When God decides that the human experiment has gone on long enough, yes, even in the midst of what appears to us confusion and incompleteness, Christ will come again.

This is what the New Testament teaches. This is the message of Advent. It is for us to be alert, vigilant and industrious, so that his coming will not be a terror but an overwhelming joy.

From 'The Christian Year' from *Good News: Thoughts on God and Man*, The Macmillan Co, New York, 1963.

Saturday of the fourth week of Advent

World-Mothering God
Sergius Bulgakov

In dogmatic terms, Mary's link to the divine may be expressed as a special connection with the Holy Spirit. The archangel's words at the annunciation are explicit about this: 'The Holy Spirit will come upon you, and the power of the Most High will overshadow you' (Lk 1:35). Through the Spirit's visitation Mary became Mother of God. Her moral purity and receptivity made her 'transparent for the Holy Spirit'. The permeation of Mary's being by the Spirit was so complete that she should be regarded not just as a supremely 'spiritual' person but as 'The Spirit-bearing Person'. Mary received the Holy Spirit with her whole being and bore its unique gift – the Son – into the world. She was the 'Spirit-bearer', the Spirit's 'living abode' in the world.

This suggests an analogy between Mary and John the Forerunner: as the friend of the bridegroom received the Second Person of the Trinity into the world, so Mary, the friend of the Holy Spirit, received the Third Person of the Trinity. As the humanity of the Holy Spirit, Mary is the perfectly sanctified, revivified, deified human being, to such a degree that her mortal flesh is glorified and assumed into heaven. But Mary does not anticipate Jesus' work any more than Jesus recapitulates hers. Their missions are distinct, though co-ordinated and equally integral to the humanity of God.

A restored humanity in the image of the Holy Trinity

will therefore manifest both the humanity of God and the motherhood of God as in the icon of the Mother of God with her child.

Mary is the perfect image of the Holy Spirit. The Spirit gives life, the Spirit sanctifies. In both respects the Spirit's work may be described as a kind of mothering. Even in the inner life of the Trinity the Spirit has a maternal function and is a life-giving and life-nurturing force far vaster than the motherhood of Mary, although the latter is the perfect creaturely image of it. The work of the Spirit is nothing less than a kind of universal, cosmic motherhood of God. Annunciation looks ahead to Pentecost and beyond when creation will appear as Christ in the process of being born, human existence as the God-bearing womb, the whole world as the Mother of God.

Unlike the Son the Spirit knows no Ascension but stays in the world to effect 'the continuing Pentecost'. To see the Spirit at work one must look to where that work is going on, namely, to the unfolding world-historical process.

From *Modern Russian Theology: Bukharev, Soloviev, Bulgakov, Orthodox Theology in a new key,* Paul Valliere, T & T Clark, Edinburgh, 2000. Used by kind permission of Continuum International Publishing Group Ltd.

The Feast of the Immaculate Conception

Symphony of the Blessed
Hildegard of Bingen

Then I saw the lucent sky, in which I heard different kinds
of music, marvellously embodying all the meanings I had
heard before. I heard the praises of the joyous citizens of
heaven, whose song, like the voice of a multitude singing in
harmony, had these words as songs to holy Mary:

O splendid jewel, serenely infused with the Sun!
The Sun is in you as a fount from the heart of the Father;
It is His sole Word, by Whom He created the world,
The primary matter, which Eve threw into disorder.
He formed the Word in you as a human being,
And therefore you are the jewel that shines most brightly,
Through whom the Word breathed out the whole of the
virtues
As once from primary matter He made all creatures.

O sweet green branch that flowers from the stem of Jesse!
O glorious thing, that God on His fairest daughter
Looked as the eagle looks on the face of the sun!
The Most High Father sought for a Virgin's candour,
And willed that His Word should take in her His body.
For the Virgin's mind was by His mystery illumined,
And from her virginity sprang the glorious Flower.

O noble verdure, which grows from the Sun of splendour!
Your clear serenity shines in the Wheel of Godhead,
Your greatness is past all earthly understanding,
And Heaven's wonders surround you in their embrace.
You glow like dawn and burn like the Sun in glory.

From Vision Thirteen, *Scivias*, The Classics of Western Spirituality, Paulist Press, New York, 1990. Used by kind permission of the publishers.

The Season of Christmas

Christmas Vigil

O Christian, be aware of your nobility
Pope St Leo the Great

My friends, this is the day our Saviour was born: let us rejoice and give thanks. This is no season for sadness, this, the birthday of Life. Life removes all fear of death, giving birth to the joy of immortality.

No one is a stranger to this happiness. The same cause for joy is common to us all. No one of us was free from guilt when the Saviour removed our chains. His salvation from sin and death was offered to all without exception. Let the saint rejoice who hastens towards heaven; let the sinner rejoice for pardon has been won; let those who feel excluded too rejoice at this untrammelled call to life and freedom.

When the fullness of time had come, chosen in God's inscrutable wisdom, the only Son of God became himself a human being, to realign us with God's plan. Thus would the devil, father of death, be overcome by that same human nature which he himself had overcome.

Angels rejoice at the birth of the Lord, singing: 'Glory to God in high heaven and peace to his people on earth.' If angels sing for joy because they see the heavenly Jerusalem being built from every tribe and tongue and people and nation, how much more exultantly should we not rejoice over this amazing display of God's love on our behalf?

My friends, let us give thanks to God the Father, through his Son, in the Holy Spirit, whose tender compassion so overwhelms us, that in giving life to Christ they give us life too, making a new creation out of our humanity, a new work of their own hands.

Let us leave behind us, the self we used to be, with all that held us back or held us down. As newborn sharers in the life of Christ let us break with our former way of life and live with him.

O Christian, be aware of your nobility – you now share in God's own nature: do not fall back into your former way of life. Remember the head, remember the body to which you now belong. Remember that you have been removed from the threshold of darkness and made welcome in a household of light and of love.

Through the waters of baptism the Holy Spirit has made of you a temple. Do not forfeit your freedom by turning yourself once more into a slave. Remember that you were ransomed at the price of Christ's blood.

Sermo XXI, In Nativitate, Domini Nostri Jesu Christi, I. [Migne PL 54 Col. 64-66]

Christmas Day

Christmas
Karl Rahner

God has come. He is here in the world. And therefore everything is different from what we imagine it to be. Time is transformed from its eternal flow into an event that with silent, clear resoluteness leads to a definitely determined goal wherein we and the world shall stand before the unveiled face of God. When we say, 'It is Christmas,' we mean that God has spoken into the world his last, his deepest, his most beautiful word in the incarnate Word, a word that can no longer be revoked because it is God's definitive deed, because it is God himself in the world.

And this word means: I love you, you, the world and humankind. This is a wholly unexpected word, a quite unlikely word. For how can this word be spoken when both humankind and the world are recognised as dreadful, empty abysses? But God knows them better than we. And yet he has spoken this word by being himself born as a creature. The very existence of this incarnate Word of love demands that it shall provide, eye to eye and heart to heart, an almost unbelievable fellowship, an *admirabile commercium*, between the eternal God and us. Indeed, it says that this *commercium* is already there. This is the word that God has spoken in the birth of his Son.

And now there is stillness in the world only for a little while. The busyness that is proudly called universal history, or one's own life, is only the strategem of an eternal love that wills to enable us to give a free answer to its final word. And in this prolonged short moment of God's silence that is called history after the birth of Christ, we are supposed to have a chance to speak. In the trembling of my heart that quivers because of God's love, I should tell God, who as a human person stands beside me in silent expectation, 'I' – no, rather say nothing to him, but silently give yourself to the love of God that is there because the Son is born.

From, *The Eternal Year*, Burns & Oates, London, 1964. Used by kind permission of Continuum International Publishing Group Ltd.

Reading for The Day after Christmas

St Stephen
Vincent Ryan

We are within the octave of Christmas and our focus of attention is 'the new-born Christ'. But Stephen is foremost among the *comites Christi*, the 'companions/fellow-travellers of Christ', as they were known in the Middle Ages. The cluster of saints' days around the feast of Christmas forms a kind of guard-of-honour to the one born to be King.

All we know about St Stephen is derived from chapter six of the Acts of the Apostles. He was one of seven deacons chosen to minister to the Greek-speaking Christians in Jerusalem. Deacons were responsible for distributing alms as well as exercising a ministry of preaching. Stephen, 'blessed by God and full of power', performed miracles among the people. The Spirit dwelling in him gave him courage and eloquence in bearing witness to Jesus. He was stoned to death for his profession of faith and is venerated as the first martyr.

The liturgy makes play of Stephen's name. *Stephanos* means a crown or wreath. In ancient Greece a laurel wreath, symbolising victory, was given to champions in athletic contests. Stephen's victory was of a spiritual kind, one of faith and love. 'Today Christ has crowned St Stephen', declares the invitatory antiphon. Likewise St Fulgentius can declare: 'St Stephen, so as to deserve to win the crown, which is what his name means, had love as his weapon, and by it was everywhere victorious.'

Christ's self-sacrificing death was a victory of light over darkness, of love over hatred. St Stephen closely resembled his master in the manner of his dying. He too prayed for his enemies: 'Lord, do not hold this sin against them.' Christ committed his soul to the Father, Stephen committed his to Jesus: 'Lord Jesus, receive my spirit.'

'Love your enemies and pray for those who persecute you', Jesus demands of his disciples in the Sermon on the Mount (Mt 5:44). It may seem an unreasonable, even an impossible request. But Jesus practised what he preached, as did his first martyr. The church, faithful to the teaching and example of Christ, has always prayed for its enemies, not that they remain enemies but rather that they undergo a change of heart, that they be converted and live. In the Our Father the petition for forgiveness of our own sins is conditional on our readiness to forgive others. Among the oldest forms of liturgical intercession we find prayers 'for the enemies of the church'. Tradition has it that Stephen's dying prayer won the grace of conversion for the young Saul who was a witness and accomplice to his murder but who was destined to become Paul the Apostle and Teacher of the Nations. In the Byzantine Liturgy the faithful are enjoined to 'pray for those who love us and those who hate us'. The heroic example of the church's protomartyr urges us in our turn to pray today: 'Give us grace, Lord, to practise what we worship. Teach us to love our enemies as we keep the feast of St Stephen who prayed even for those who stoned him.'

27 December: Feast of St John the Evangelist

The Voice of the Eagle

John Scotus Eriugena's homily
on the prologue to the gospel of St John

The spiritual bird, fast-flying, God-seeing – I mean John, the theologian – ascends beyond all visible and invisible creation, passes through all thought and intellect, and, deified, enters into God who deifies him.

O Blessed Paul, you were caught up, as you yourself assert, into the third heaven, to paradise; but you were not caught up beyond every heaven and every paradise created, beyond every human and angelic nature.

In the third heaven, O vessel of election and teacher of the gentiles, you heard words not lawful for a human being to utter. But John, the observer of the inmost truth, in the paradise of paradises, in the very cause of all, heard the one Word through which all things are made.

It was permitted to him to speak this Word, and to proclaim it, as far as it may be proclaimed, to human beings. Therefore most confidently he cried out, 'In the beginning was the Word.'

John, therefore, was not a human being but more than a human being when he flew above himself and all things that are. Transported by the ineffable power of wisdom and by the purest keenness of mind, he entered that which is beyond all things: namely, the secret of the single essence in three substances and the three substances in the single essence.

He would not have been able to ascend into God if he had not first become God. Thus the holy theologian, transmuted into God, and participating in the truth, proclaims that God, the Word, subsists in God, the Father.

Behold heaven opened and the mystery of the highest and holiest Trinity revealed!

'In the beginning was the Word … and the Word was made flesh.'

From *The Voice of the Eagle*, trs Christopher Bamford, Lindisfarne Books, USA, New Edition, 2001, pp 75-77. Used by kind permission of the publisher.

28 December

The Holy Innocents
John Henry Newman

The longer we live in the world, and the further removed we are from the feelings and remembrances of childhood (and especially if removed from the sight of children), the more reason we have to recollect our Lord's impressive action and word, when he called a little child unto him, and set him in the midst of his disciples, and said, 'Verily I say unto you, except ye be converted, and become as little children, ye shall not enter into the kingdom of heaven.'

It is surely right and meet to celebrate the death of the Holy Innocents: for it was a blessed one. Surely this massacre had in it the nature of a sacrament; it was a pledge of the love of the Son of God towards those who were included in it. Hence in ancient times such barbarous murders or martyrdoms were considered as a kind of baptism, a baptism of blood, with a sacramental charm in it, which stood in the place of the appointed Laver of regeneration. Let us then take these little children as in some sense martyrs, and see what instruction we may gain from the pattern of their innocence.

There is very great danger of our becoming cold-hearted, as life goes on: afflictions which happen to us, cares, disappointments, all tend to blunt our affections and make our feelings callous. There is in most minds a secret instinct of reverence and affection towards the days of childhood. They cannot help sighing with regret and tenderness when they think of it. If we wish to affect a person, what can we do better than appeal to the memory of times past, and above all to his childhood! There is in the infant soul, in the first years of its regenerate state, a discernment of the unseen world in the things that are seen, a realisation of what is Sovereign and Adorable, and an incredulity and ignorance about what is transient and changeable, which mark it as the fit emblem of the matured Christian, when weaned from things temporal, and living in the intimate conviction of the Divine Presence. The simplicity of a child's ways and notions, their ready belief of everything they are told, their artless love, their frank confidence, their confession of help-lessness, their ignorance of evil, their inability to conceal their thoughts, their contentment, their prompt forgetful-ness of trouble, their admiring without coveting; and, above all, their reverential spirit, looking at all things about them as wonderful, as tokens and types of the One Invisible, are all evidence of their being lately (as it were) visitants in a higher state of things. And though, doubtless, all children are not equally amiable, yet their passions go and are over like a shower; not interfering with the lesson we may gain to our own profit from their ready faith and guilelessness. How striking a pattern a child's mind gives us of what may be called a church temper.

From *Parochial and Plain Sermons*, Volume 2, No 6.

29 December

Of Gold, Frankincense and Myrrh
Edith Stein

Mary and Joseph are not to be separated from their Divine
Child in the Christmas liturgy. During this time they do
not have a feast of their own because all the feasts of the
Lord are their feasts, feasts of the Holy Family. They do not
come to the manger, they are there to begin with. Whoever
comes to the Child also comes to them.

Closest to the newborn Saviour we find St Stephen.
What secured the first martyr this place of honour? He
practised complete obedience, rooted and revealed in love.
The Child in the manger points him out to us as if to say,
'See the gold I expect of you.' Not far from the first martyr
stand the defenceless lambs, the holy innocents, led to the
slaughter. They represent the utmost poverty. They have no
other goods than their lives. They surround the manger to
show us the kind of myrrh we should bring to the Divine
Child. Those who want to belong to him must deliver
themselves to him in complete self-renunciation.

Nor will the Saviour allow the one who was particularly
dear to him during his life, the disciple whom Jesus loved,
to be absent from the manger. He is entrusted to us as the
example of virginal purity. Because he was pure he was
allowed to rest on the heart of Jesus to be initiated there
into the secrets of the Divine Heart. As the heavenly Father
witnessed to his Son, in the words: 'This is My beloved
Son, listen to him!', so the Divine Child seems to point to

the beloved disciple and to say: 'No frankincense is more pleasing to me than the loving submission of a pure heart. Listen to him who was permitted to look at God because he was pure of heart.' No one has looked more deeply into the hidden abyss of divine life and love than he. Therefore, he proclaims the mystery of the Divine Word in the liturgy each feastday during the days of Christmas. We can learn from John how precious human souls are to the Divine Heart and how we can give him no greater joy than by being willing instruments to his shepherding way. John at the manger of the Lord says to us: 'See what happens to those who give themselves to God with pure hearts. In return, as a royal gift, they may participate in the entire inexhaustible fullness of Jesus' incarnate life.' We may come to him and bring him the gifts of our holy vows, gold, frankincense and myrrh. And then, in a new year, we shall go with him the entire way of his life on earth.

A new year at the hand of the Lord – we do not know whether we shall experience the end of this year. But if we drink from the fount of the Saviour each day, then each day will lead us deeper into eternal life and prepare us to throw off the burdens of this life easily and cheerfully at whatever time the call of the Lord sounds.

30 December

The Incarnation
John Henry Newman

In the New Testament we find the doctrine of the Incarnation announced clearly indeed, but with a reverent brevity. 'The Word was made flesh.'

Time having proceeded, and the true traditions of our Lord's ministry being lost to us, the Object of our faith is but faintly reflected on our minds, compared with the vivid picture which his presence impressed upon the early Christians. True is it the gospels will do very much by way of realising for us the incarnation of the Son of God, if studied in faith and love. But the Creeds are an additional help this way. The declarations made in them, the distinctions, cautions, and the like, supported and illuminated by scripture, draw down, as it were, from heaven, the image of him who is on God's right hand, preserve us from an indolent use of words without apprehending them, and rouse in us those mingled feelings of fear and confidence, affection and devotion towards him, which are implied in the belief of a personal advent of God in our nature, and which were originally derived to the church from the very sight of him.

And we may say further still, these statements – such, for instance, as occur in the *Te Deum* and Athanasian Creed – are especially suitable in divine worship, inasmuch as they kindle and elevate the religious affections. They are hymns of praise and thanksgiving; they give glory to God as revealed in the gospel, just as David's psalms magnify his attributes as displayed in nature, his wonderful works in the creation of the world, and his mercies towards the house of Israel.

The Word was from the beginning, the Only-begotten Son of God. Before all worlds were created, while as yet time was not, he was in existence, in the bosom of the Eternal Father, God from God, and Light from Light, supremely blessed in knowing and being known of him, and receiving all divine perfections from him, yet ever One with him who begat him. As it is said in the opening of the gospel: 'In the beginning was the Word, and the Word was with God, and the Word was God.' He, indeed, when we fell, might have remained in the glory which he had with the Father before the world was. But that unsearchable Love, which showed itself in our original creation, rested not content with a frustrated work, but brought him down again from his Father's bosom to do his will, and repair the evil which sin had caused. And with a wonderful con-descension he came, not as before in power, but in weakness, in the form of a servant, in the likeness of that fallen creature whom he purposed to restore. So he humbled himself; suffering all the infirmities of our nature in the likeness of sinful flesh, all but a sinner – pure from all sin, yet subjected to all temptation – and at length becoming obedient unto death, even the death of the cross.

From *Parochial and Plain Sermons*, Volume 2, Sermon 3.

31 December

Prefer nothing to the love of Christ
Olivier Clément

In Christ we have everything ...
If you want to heal your wound, he is the doctor.
If you are burning with fever, he is the fountain.
If you are in need of help, he is strength.
If you are in dread of death, he is life.
If you are fleeing the darkness, he is light.
If you are hungry, he is food:
Taste and see that the Lord is good!
Happy are they who take refuge in him (Psalm 34:8)

We are called to travel this way in the Holy Spirit. For Christ's humanity is the scene of an unending Pentecost. In Christ we can receive the Spirit fully, drink the 'living water,' the 'water welling up to eternal life'.

'The Word made himself "bearer of the flesh" in order that human beings might become "bearers of the Spirit".'

A stream has welled up, it has become a torrent ...
It has flooded the universe, it has converged on the temple.
No bank or dam could halt it ...
It has spread over the whole face of the earth and replenished it completely.
All who were thirsty have drunk of it and their thirst has been quenched,
For the Most High has given them to drink.

By means of the living water they live forever.
The Holy Spirit is inseparable from our freedom. God
remains in history the beggar who waits at each person's
gate with infinite patience, begging for love. His silence,
with which we sometimes reproach him, only shows his
consideration for us. The cross and the resurrection coexist.
'Christ will be in agony to the very end of the world,' he
will suffer, according to Origen, until all humanity has
entered the kingdom.

From *The Roots of Christian Mysticism*, New City, New York. Used
by kind permission of the publishers.

Sunday after Christmas: Feast of The Holy Family

The Holy Family
Geoffrey Preston

We have to break with our families if we are to find ourselves.
In the story of the losing and finding of the boy Jesus in
the Temple the major obstacle to the journey of Jesus
appears to have been all that is meant by 'family'. Family
gets Jesus to Jerusalem in the first place, but it also tries to
recover him prematurely once he has arrived. The day will
come when it will try to prevent him from returning there
when it really matters.

The experience that the *familiar* gets in the way is
common to very many Christians. House, brothers, sisters,
father, mother, children, are part of what Peter and the others
had to leave in order to follow Jesus. The pattern goes back
to Abraham, who had to leave his father's house and it goes
on to our own time. It is the pattern of the dark night of
mysticism and of the dark night of political involvement.

Families are not ultimates. Of course, there can be no
excuse for not following the Christian ways of justice and
love with our families: but still they are not absolutes. There
is nothing absolute about a family, not a biological family
nor those families which are our local and national institutions, nor even the religious communities which have
adopted us and which we have chosen to make our families.
Neither blood nor soil, neither nature nor nurture, can be
allowed to have the last word in deciding who we are to
be. We are not to allow any family to displace our direct
and immediate relationship with God.

The pilgrimage of Jesus led him to this discovery in the Jerusalem Temple when he was twelve years old. He found out that there was a higher claim on him than the claims of Mary and Joseph.

For us, too, there is an inbuilt principle of unpredictability in the Word of God. It can call us to something for which we are not programmed by our families, by all that is familiar to us. When it does call us, then we have to choose to save our lives or lose them, to remain settled or to involve ourselves with the destiny of Jesus Christ. We have to distance ourselves from even the holiest of things for the sake of God, as Jesus distanced himself even from Mary and Joseph. The first great break-up occurs when Jesus at twelve years old contrasts the One he calls his Father with the one Mary calls his father. 'Your father and I have sought you sorrowing.' 'Did you not know,' Jesus replies 'that I must be in my Father's house, and about my Father's business?'

This is a move which all Christians must make: 'Call no man your father on earth, for only one is your Father, the heavenly One.' We may not define ourselves in terms of even the highest of categories, the most godly of institutions. Home, in all this, is more a symbol than a place, more a state of mind than a building. Home is where we feel at home; and God seems to have difficulty in dealing with us until this power of the familiar has been broken.

From *Hallowing the Time*, DLT, 1980. Used by kind permission of the publisher.

1 January: Solemnity of Mary, Mother of God

Becoming the Mother of God
Hans Urs von Balthasar

At the point where all roads meet which lead from the Old Testament to the New, we encounter the Marian experience of God, at once so rich and so secret that it almost escapes description. But it is also so important that time and again it shines through as the background for what is manifest.

In Mary, Zion passes over into the church; in her, the Word passes over into flesh. The Incarnation of the Word occurs in the faith of the virgin. She relies not so much on the appearance of the angel as on his word, which is a Word from God. The lightning-flash of the miracle has no counterpart in her human experience; this experience begins afterwards, as a temporal echo of this miracle. It begins with a blind sense of touch, with the bodily sensing of a presence – the sense of touch as the fundamental, unerring sense – and this experience intensifies first within its own particular kind before it extends to embrace also the experience of seeing and hearing which comes with the birth. The gradual separation into two, of the one natural consciousness of the body at that stage when the mother's consciousness still embraces both bodies, is like an imitation, within the economy of salvation, of the mystery of the Trinity, and, no less, like an imitation (the first and the closest imitation) of the mystery of the two natures in the one Person. The mother is still both herself and her child.

Seen in the light of Mary's simple experience of motherhood, which in her has become a function of the archetypal act of faith, all closed consciousness of self and all closed experience of self become problematic: the experience of self must open out, through faith, to an experience that encompasses both oneself and the other – oneself and the burgeoning Word of God. At first, as with Mary, this seems to be growing in the self, until in this very growth it becomes evident that it is the other way round: it is the self that is contained in the Word of God.

From *The Glory of The Lord, Vol. I: Theological Aesthetics*, T&T Clark, 1982. Used by kind permission of Continuum International Publishing Group.

Second Sunday after Christmas

Christ, True and Perfect Man
Anthony Bloom

The Incarnation, the fact that God became human, is a
revelation both of God and of humanity. In order to understand, therefore, how fully we are revealed through the
Incarnation, one must rediscover how fully God is revealed.
The gods of antiquity, of philosophical discourse, were
always images of the greatness of humanity or of the greatness which humanity could perceive or imagine in a super-
human being. What no religion, no philosophy, ever dared
present was a god who becomes human, suffers and empties
himself of his splendour in order to become fully and completely accessible to us. In the Incarnation we discover that
our God, the Holy One of Israel, the Creator of the world,
the Beauty that surpasses all beauty, the Truth and the only
Reality of the world – that this God chooses, in an act of
love, so to identify himself with the destinies of
humankind, so to take upon himself total and ultimate
responsibility for his creative act, that all the beauty of the
world is called forth, while at the same time he gives the
world the freedom that destroys and distorts this beauty.
This God who chooses to become frail, vulnerable,
defenceless and contemptible in the eyes of all those who
believe only in strength, in power and in visible temporal
victory – such a god a devout, believing person could not
have invented. To conceive of a god in such terms would
have been blasphemy. And yet. God reveals himself as such:

vulnerable, defenceless, frail and contemptible. This is the folly of the Cross of which St Paul speaks. And the folly is not only ours; it is the folly of God as well. A certain number of mystics speak of divine Love as being folly, because to offer love to creatures like us, who may be incapable of responding, who may reject it and trample it underfoot as the swine trample the pearl of great price in the parable, is folly. But then, as St Paul says, the folly of God is wiser than the wisdom of humankind. Angelus Silesius, the German mystic, says: 'I am as great as God; he is as small as I.' We need to think about what this means.

This address was delivered at the Diocesan Conference at Effingham, Surrey, in May 1983.

2 January

The Incarnation
Hans Urs von Balthasar

The Incarnation of the Word means the most extreme
manifestness within the deepest concealment. It is manifestness because here God is explained to humanity by no
means other than humanity itself – not primarily through
words and instruction, but by human being and human life.
What is most familiar to us is suddenly turned for us into a
word and a teaching about God: how could we not
understand!

But it is concealment because the translation of God's
absolutely unique, absolute, and infinite Being into the ever
more dissimilar, almost arbitrary and hopelessly relativised
reality of one individual human being in the crowd, from
the outset appears to be an undertaking condemned to failure.
For, if 'man' is truly to become the language of God, this
cannot occur by straining human nature towards the super-
human, or by wishing to stand out by becoming greater,
more splendid, more renowned and more stupendous than
all others. He will have to be a man *like* everyone because
he will be man *for* everyone, and he will exhibit his
uniqueness precisely through his ordinariness: 'He will not
wrangle or cry aloud, nor will anyone hear his voice in the
busy streets' (Is 42:2=Mt 12:19). The insignificant must be
the appearance of what is most significant. We could
understand it better if the hiddenness of this 'flesh' were
supposed to represent the silence of the Word, God's pure

concealment. But no: precisely this hiddenness is to be the speech in which God desires to make himself known definitively and insurpassably, beyond misunderstanding or confusion with any other human word.

Here we once again encounter the difficulty of the revelation of the Word. This revelation does not have its place alongside the revelation in the creation, as if it competed with it, but within it. In the same way, the revelation in the Incarnation has its place within the revelation of God's Being in man, who as God's image and likeness, conceals God even as he reveals him. This means that, in Christ, humanity is disclosed along with God. God does not use human nature like an external instrument to articulate, from the outside and from above, the Wholly Other which God is; rather, God takes on human nature as his own and expresses himself from within it through the expressive structures of that nature's essence. The Creator does not misuse his own creation for a purpose alien to it, rather, by his becoming man, he honours it and crowns it and brings it to its own most intimate perfection. God is able, therefore, to reveal in Christ, at once God and humanity, and this is not in alteration, as is often suggested simplistically, but simultaneously. Yet this occurs in such a way that the relativity of the human does not appear to be oppressed and violated by the simultaneous absoluteness of the divine.

From *The Glory of The Lord, Vol. I: Theological Aesthetics*, T&T Clark, 1982. Used by kind permission of Continuum International Publishing Group.

3 January

Christ the Centre
Hans Urs von Balthasar

The fact that Christ is the centre of the form of revelation
– and not, for instance, merely the beginning, the initiator
of an historical form which then develops autonomously –
is rooted in the particular character of the Christian religion
and in its difference from all other religions. Judaism has no
such centre: neither Abraham, nor Moses, nor one of the
Prophets, is the figure around which everything else is
ordered. Christ, by contrast, is the form because he is the
content. This holds absolutely, for he is the only Son of the
Father, and whatever he establishes and institutes has its
meaning only through him, is dependent only on him and
is kept vital only by him. If for a single moment we were to
look away from him and attempt to consider and understand
the church as an autonomous form, the church would not
have the slightest plausibility. It would be plausible neither
as a religious institution nor as an historical power for order
and culture. On the contrary, seen in this way it loses all
credibility, and for this reason the church Fathers often
compared the church's light with the light of the moon,
borrowed from the sun and showing its relativity most
clearly in its phases. The plausibility of Christianity stands
and falls with Christ's, something which has in essence
always been acknowledged.

    The form that we encounter historically is convincing
in itself because the light by which it illumines radiates
from the form itself and proves itself with compelling force

to be just such a light that springs from the object itself.

The fact that Christ 'says nothing to me' in no way prejudices the fact that, in and of himself, Christ says everything to everyone. What is at stake here is the correspondence of human existence as a whole to the form of Christ. Not only intellectual but also existential prerequisites must be fulfilled in order that the form that makes its claim on one's total existence may also find a hearing in this total existence.

If the form of Christ itself is what it shows itself to be of itself, then no particular age or culture can of itself be privileged in repect of this phenomenon. The decisively illuminating factor must lie in the phenomenon itself, and this in two senses. First, in the sense that the figure which Christ forms has in itself an interior rightness and evidential power such as we find – in another, wholly worldly realm – in a work of art or in a mathematical principle. And, second, in the sense that this rightness, which resides within the reality of the thing itself, also possesses the power to illumine the perceiving person by its own radiant light, and this not simply intellectually but in a way that transforms our existence. The gospel presents Christ's form in such a way that 'flesh' and 'spirit', Incarnation to the point of suffering and death, and resurrected life are all interrelated down to the smallest details. Each element is plausible only within the wholeness of the image.

From *The Glory of The Lord, Vol I: Theological Aesthetics*, T&T Clark, 1982. Used by kind permission of Continuum International Publishing Group.

4 January

The Epiphany
John Henry Newman

The Epiphany is a season especially set apart for adoring the glory of Christ. The word may be taken to mean the manifestation of his glory, and leads us to the contemplation of him as a King upon his throne. At Christmas we commemorate his grace; and in Lent his temptation; and on Good Friday his sufferings and death; and on Easter Day his victory; and on Holy Thursday his return to the Father; and in Advent we anticipate his second coming. And in all of these seasons he does something, or suffers something: but in the Epiphany and the weeks after it, we celebrate him, not as on his field of battle, or in his solitary retreat, but as an august and glorious King.

As great men of this world are often plainly dressed, and look like other men, all but as having some one costly ornament on their breast or on their brow; so the Son of Mary in his lowly dwelling, and in an infant's form, was declared to be the Son of God Most High, the Father of Ages, and the Prince of Peace, by his star; a wonderful appearance which had guided the wise men all the way from the East, even unto Bethlehem.

There is no thought of war, or of strife, or of suffering, or of triumph, or of vengeance connected with the Epiphany, but of august majesty, of power, of prosperity, of splendour, of serenity, of benignity.

When he is with the doctors in the temple, he is manifested as a prophet – in turning the water into wine, as a priest – in his miracles of healing, as a bounteous Lord, giving out of his abundance – in his rebuking the sea, as a sovereign, whose word is law – in the parable of the wheat and tares, as a guardian and ruler – in his second coming, as a lawgiver and judge.

You will observe, then, that the only display of royal greatness, the only season of majesty, homage, and glory, which our Lord had on earth, was in his infancy and youth. Gabriel's message to Mary was in its style and manner such as befitted an angel speaking to Christ's mother. Elisabeth, too, saluted Mary, and the future Baptist his hidden Lord, in the same honourable way. Angels announced his birth, and the shepherds worshipped. A star appeared, and the wise men rose from the East and made him offerings. He was brought to the temple, and Simeon took him in his arms, and returned thanks for him. He grew to twelve years old, and again he appeared in the temple, and took his seat in the midst of the doctors. But here his earthly majesty had its end. We are told at the close of the last-mentioned narrative, 'And he went down with his parents, and came to Nazareth, and was subjected unto them' (Lk 2:51). His subjection and servitude now began in fact. He had come in the form of a servant, and now he took on him a servant's office. How much is contained in the idea of his subjection! And it began, and his time of glory ended, when he was twelve years old.

From *Parochial and Plain Sermons*, Volume 7, Sermon 6.

5 January

The Epiphany
Karl Rahner

One of the names given to this feast, to this 'supreme day' (as the Middle Ages called it,) is 'The Feast of the Three Kings'. Untheological and unhistorical this cherished name for the feast may be, because the Wise Men at the crib neither constitute the subject matter of the feast, nor were they kings, nor were there, for sure, even three of them; yet the name 'Three Kings' points out a significant aspect of the feast's mystery: that the first people on earth searched everywhere for the child who would redeem them, roving like pilgrims, journeying from afar through every kind of danger. So this day is the feastday of all those who seek God through their life's pilgrimage, the journey of those who find God because they seek God. When we read of the Magi in the first twelve verses of the second chapter of St Matthew, we are reading our own story, the history of our own pilgrimage. Led by a star, these Magi from far off Persia struggled through deserts and successfully questioned their way through indifference and politics until they found the child and could worship him as Saviour-King.

Somewhere and at some time we come into existence. The journey's path moves through childhood, through youthfulness, through maturity, through a few festive days and many routine days. It moves through heights and through misery, through purity and through sin, through love and through disillusionment. On and on it goes, irresistibly from the morning of life to the evening of death.

But where does the journey lead? Did we find ourselves – when we awoke to our existence – placed in a procession that goes on and on without our knowing where it is leading, so that we have only to settle down and get accustomed to this motion, learn to tolerate it, and conduct ourselves in an orderly and peaceful fashion, and not dare to consult God's will to find out where this procession is really going? Or do we actually look to find a goal on this journey, because our secret heart knows that there is such a goal, however difficult and long the road might be?

We know very well that God is the goal of our pilgrimage. God dwells in the remote distance. The way to God seems to us all too far and all too hard. And what we ourselves mean when we say 'God' is incomprehensible. The free spirit finds only what it looks for. But God has promised in his word that he lets himself be found by those who seek him. In grace he wills to be not merely the one who is always a little farther beyond every place that the creature on pilgrimage has reached, but rather to be that one who really can be found, eye to eye, heart to heart, by those small creatures with an eternal heart that we call human beings.

From, *The Eternal Year*, Burns & Oates, London, 1964. Used by kind permission of Continuum International Publishing Group Ltd.

6 January

The Epiphany
Karl Rahner

Behold, the wise men have set out. For their heart was on pilgrimage towards God when their feet pointed towards Bethlehem. They sought him; but he was already leading them because they sought him. They are the type of those who yearn for salvation, yearn in hunger and thirst for righteousness. That is why they did not think they could dare omit this one step forward just because God has to take a thousand in order for both to meet. They were looking for him, for salvation, in the heavens and in their hearts. They saw a strange star rise in the heavens. And God in his kindness allowed their astrology, foolish though it may be, to succeed this once, because their pure hearts did not know any better.

Their hearts must have trembled a little when the theory drawn from their obscure knowledge of the Jewish expectation of salvation, and from their astrology, should now suddenly become applied in practice in a very concrete journey. Their bold hearts must have been a little frightened. They might almost have preferred that their hearts not take so seriously noble principles so foreign to reality and so impractical. But the heart is strong and courageous. They obeyed their hearts, and they set out.

And suddenly, as they left their native land behind, at the moment they dared to leap into a hazardous venture, their hearts became light, like the heart of one who has ventured all and is more courageous than is really possible.

They travelled over tortuous paths, but in God's eyes their path led straight to him because they sought him in sincerity. It frightened them to be so far from their familiar native country, but they knew that in journeying everything has to be transformed, and they marched on and on in order to find the native land that would be more than a tent by the wayside. They knew from their own deeds (life is more than the mind's theories) that to live means that we are always changing, and that perfection means passing through many levels of change.

They do not know where the courage and the strength keep coming from. It is not from themselves, and it just suffices; but it never fails as long as one does not ask and does not peer inquisitively into the empty reaches of the heart to see if something is inside, but bravely keeps on spending the mysterious contents of the heart.

And when they came and knelt down, they only did what they had in reality always been doing, what they were already doing during their search and journey: they brought before the face of the invisible God now made visible, the gold of their love, the incense of their reverence and the myrrh of their suffering.

From, *The Eternal Year*, Burns & Oates, London, 1964. Used by kind permission of Continuum International Publishing Group Ltd.

Monday after Epiphany

Christmas Sermon
Johann Tauler

It is certain that if God is to be born in the soul
It must turn back to eternity
It must turn in towards itself with all its might,
Must recall itself,
And consecrate all its faculties within itself,
The lowest as well as the highest,
All its dissipated powers must be gathered up into one,
Because unity is strength.

Next the soul must go out.
It must travel away from itself, above itself.
There must be nothing left in us
but a pure intention towards God;
no will to be or become or obtain anything for ourselves.
We must exist only to make place for him,
The highest inmost place,
Where he may do his work;
There, when we are no longer putting ourselves in his way,
He can be born in us.

If one would prepare an empty place
In the depths of the soul
There can be no doubt that God must fill it at once.
If there were void on earth
The heavens would fall to fill it.
So you must be silent.

Then God will be born in you,
Utter his word in you
And you shall hear it;
But be very sure that if you speak
The word will have to be silent.
If you go out, he will most surely come in;
As much as you go out for him
He will come to you;
No more, no less.

When shall we find and know
this birth of God within us?
Only when we concentrate
all our faculties within us
and direct them all towards God.
Then he will be born in us
and make himself our very own.
He will give himself to us as our own,
more completely ours
than anything we ever called our own.

The text says: 'A child is born to us and a son is given to us.'
He is ours
He is all our own,
more truly than anything else we own,
and constantly, ceaselessly, he is born in us.

From *Spiritual Conferences*, B. Herder Book Co, London, 1961 pp 156-158.

Tuesday after Epiphany

Three Great Wonders
Peter Henrici

'Three great wonders sanctify this day: Today the star guided
the Wise Men to the Child in the crib. Today water became
wine at the wedding feast. Today Christ our salvation was
baptised in the Jordan.' Thus sings the liturgy of the church
in the Office of Vespers for the sixth of January, the Feast of
the Lord's Epiphany. This threefold 'today' is somewhat
confusing since it encompasses a period of thirty years and
does not even reflect the actual chronology of events. And
the corresponding antiphon from Lauds of the same feast of
the Epiphany only adds to the confusion: 'Today the church
was wedded to the heavenly bridegroom. In the Jordan,
Christ washed her clean of her sins. The Wise Men hurry
with gifts to the wedding of the king. Water is transformed
into wine and gladdens the guests.'

One thing is clear about the liturgy's interweaving of
these three temporally distant events: the wedding at Cana
has a much greater significance in the liturgy than it does
in the mind of the average Christian. John's account of
Cana belongs, it is true, to the most accessible passages of
the gospel; it has a human appeal that has made it the
inspiration for countless artists and poets. And yet, little
notice is given to the fundamental significance for our faith
of this 'mystery of the life of Jesus'. Every 'mystery' is a real,
experienceable occurrence in which something of God's
hidden glory comes to light – for all those who have eyes
to see and ears to hear.

The symbolic content of the miraculous transformation of wine lends the celebration of the wedding feast a deeper significance. The messianic age that is now being ushered in must be understood as Yahweh's nuptials with his people – a marriage in which Jesus and Mary play a decisive role, and in which Jesus' disciples are also present. This eschatological nuptial mystery, which is the true 'mystery' of Cana, takes place in the ordinary, inconspicuous setting of a provincial country marriage between two probably very insignificant people. This one marriage, here elevated to the real symbol of the coming of the kingdom of God, is the foundation of the sacramentality of every Christian marriage.

From 'The Miracle of Cana' in *Communio*, Spring 2006. Used by kind permission of the publisher.

Wednesday after Epiphany

What Does Liturgy Do?
Robert Taft

In the creation scene depicted in the Sistine Chapel in Rome, which Michelangelo completed in 1513, the life-giving finger of God stretches out and almost – but not quite – touches the outstretched finger of the reclining Adam. Liturgy fills the gap between these two fingers. For God in the Sistine metaphor is a creating, life-giving, saving, redeeming hand, ever reaching out towards us, and salvation history is the story of our hands raised (or refusing to be raised) in never-ending reception of, and thanksgiving for, that gift. And isn't that what liturgy is all about? That ongoing, saving, give-and-take between God and us, Jacob's ladder of salvation history.

Given by God and received by us, this experience of salvation through faith is an encounter with God, by means of God's epiphany who is Jesus Christ, continued among us today through the in-dwelling of Christ's Spirit in the community he calls his own. His action is prior: he must call. That is why the church is a 'calling together' – *ekklesia* in Greek – not a 'coming together' on our own initiative, not an 'assembly' but a 'convocation'. So he first must call. But the call must be answered. Someone has to pick up the phone.

From 'What does Liturgy Do?' *Worship* 66, no 3 (May 1992). Used by kind permission of the author.

Thursday after Epiphany

The Baptism of Jesus
Heinrich Schlier

The evangelist Matthew (3:13-17) discerned the significant baptism event in the same circumstances as Mark. But he did not see in them solely the epiphany of the hidden Messiah. In Mark no word of Jesus is reported, only his silent gaze, and the fact of baptism is simply mentioned, and appears almost incidental. Matthew, however, refers to a conversation with the Baptist. And this conversation, together with Jesus' intention of receiving baptism from John, reveals a little of the hidden Messiah.

John does not want to baptise Jesus. He recognises in him the man who will 'baptise with the Holy Spirit and with fire' (3:11) who will judge the world and bring it to its consummation. His reply to Jesus' request is that he, John, must be baptised by Jesus. But Jesus who is in fact, although this is still hidden from the eyes of the world, the ground and occasion of all ultimate decision, insists on his request, his mysterious command to John to confer on him also the baptism for sin, the baptism of conversion to God. And he gives the reason for this request in the mysterious statement, 'for thus it is fitting for us to fulfil all righteousness'. By having himself baptised, he fulfils in obedience to God 'all righteousness,' that is, the righteousness demanded by God's Torah as it was originally, when unfalsified and rightly understood (5:17) and which, therefore, is 'more' than the righteousness of the scribes and Pharisees (5:20). But how does he fulfil this righteousness by baptism? Now at the beginning of his way, on which time and time again he will stand 'with' sinners, joins them in the baptism which he asks of the Baptist. From then on, he who always comes to them as one who already stands with them, becomes more and more profoundly involved in such standing with them until it is manifest on the cross as his dying for them. And so this baptism in water by John becomes the anticipatory sign of that baptism which is his death on the cross. Mark (10:30) and Luke (12:50) also speak of this as a baptism.

From *The Relevance of the New Testament*, Burns & Oates, 1968. Used by kind permission of the Continuum International Publishing Group.

Friday after Epiphany

The Baptism of Jesus
Heinrich Schlier

The evangelist Luke follows the Marcan tradition concerning the Baptism of Jesus and makes little change in it. Nevertheless small differences from Mark show from what angle he envisaged the tradition and how he understood the baptism event and wanted it understood. He speaks of Jesus' coming to baptism 'when all the people were baptised'. He is therefore aware of Jesus' solidarity with sinners who are converted. But he does not elaborate on this. His thoughts dwell exclusively on the significant events which Mark has related and in the light of which the mysterious Messiah-Servant of God is manifest. Certainly in Luke they do not occur in such an unprepared way, nor in a way so apparently unconnected with Jesus. For in Luke we read: 'when Jesus had been baptised and was praying, the heaven opened …' It is Jesus' prayer, which Luke on other occasions also emphasises more than the other evangelists, which causes the heavens to open, the Holy Spirit to descend upon him and the divine voice to address him. And so he brings this epiphany into connection with another, that on the mountain of the transfiguration, which also took place when Jesus was praying (9:28ff). Luke sees in Jesus' baptismal epiphany a reference to his glorification. From the very beginning of his journey to Jerusalem, which of course is his 'taking up' (9:51), Jesus sets out on it as one already secretly marked out in baptism for glorification.

From *The Relevance of the New Testament*, Burns & Oates, 1968.
Used by kind permission of the Continuum International
Publishing Group.

Saturday after Epiphany

The Baptism of Jesus
Heinrich Schlier

The evangelist John's account of the baptism of Jesus is like a
medieval painting. In the foreground there still stands the
Baptist. Around him but lower than he are the people, scarcely
noticeable, because the forum he is addressing is the whole
world. The Baptist is gazing into the middle distance. There
Jesus appears and comes towards John the Baptist. Where he
comes from, no one knows. It is enough that he is coming,
coming nearer. It is not stated where he comes from.
Obviously, it is to motivate the testimony of the Baptist,
which is the essential. This testimony begins: '*Ecce agnus Dei
…*' There is already a liturgical ring about it. He who is
coming towards the Baptist is 'the Lamb', the sacrificial lamb
on which the sins of the world are laid so that it may bear
them away. The Servant of God of Isaiah 53 appears in the
light of the cross. And 'this man', who bears the burden of
the sins of the world, is the eternal Word. With him, who
appeared chronologically on the stage of history after the
Baptist, there has come he who is at all times, and with
whom the beginning and origin of all things appears
(cf 1:15). He is the eternal *Logos*, made flesh. But John the
Baptist must confess, and he confesses for us all, 'I myself did
not know him.' For in order to recognise the eternal Word,
the origin and the beginning, in Jesus who is the Lamb of
God who takes away the sins of the world, a revelation is
needed which opens the eyes of our hearts to the flesh
which brings the glory closer and at the same time hides it.

But this revelation took place. The Baptist, as he himself confesses, baptised for no other purpose than to bring it about. For at the baptism, there occurred that epiphany of Jesus narrated in the tradition which John himself had read. And it happened so that it might figure in John's testimony and so that Jesus might appear to Israel through this testimony.

From *The Relevance of the New Testament*, Burns & Oates, 1968. Used by kind permission of the Continuum International Publishing Group.

The Feast of the Baptism of the Lord

The Baptism of Jesus
Heinrich Schlier

All four gospels contain the report of Jesus' baptism. The actual act of baptism is of course simply mentioned or presupposed. The interest of the evangelists is directed to what happened in connection with the baptism. Each evangelist reports the events in his own way, each bringing out a different aspect. The church has not felt that to be a disadvantage but an enrichment.

Mark reports simply and objectively that 'in those days' – that is, when the Baptist appeared and called to penance – Jesus of Nazareth in Galilee 'came and was baptised by John in the Jordan.' The matter could hardly be related in fewer words. But that is only the introduction to what Mark finds worthy of reflection: that at this baptism there occurred the first epiphany of the Messiah-Son of God who is the Servant of God. The first epiphany of the Messianic king, not the first vision of the prophet Jesus! For Mark lays no weight on the fact that Jesus 'saw', and he makes no mention of his hearing the voice. What interests him above all, and what he wants to proclaim to Christians is, that 'the heavens opened, and the Spirit descended upon him like a dove and a voice from heaven, "Thou art my beloved Son; with whom I am well pleased".'

Since Ezechiel (1:1) the heavens opening signified the occurrence of a divine revelation. Heaven is no longer closed to earth. From the opened heaven, the Spirit appears and descends on Jesus. It is the Holy Spirit who gives access to the opened heaven of God. He descends 'like a dove' which recalls that he is the Spirit of the Creator and of the Redeemer in one. For according to the Jewish exposition of Genesis 1:2, the Spirit of God broods over the surface of the water like a dove over her young and 'the voice of the turtle dove' (song 2:12) is sometimes described as 'the voice of the Holy Spirit of redemption'.

The heavens above Jesus are torn, the Holy Spirit appears upon him, but the signs are not yet at an end. God also sends forth his voice to Jesus. In that way he inaugurates the gospel, which has no other meaning than to make it clear who this Jesus is.

From *The Relevance of the New Testament*, Burns & Oates, 1968. Used by kind permission of the Continuum International Publishing Group.

The Season of Lent

Ash Wednesday

Ash Wednesday
Karl Rahner

Dust is a good subject for reflection on Ash Wednesday, for dust, the symbol of nothingness, can tell us a great deal. The prayer that accompanies the distribution of ashes comes from Genesis (3:19): 'From the earth you were taken; dust you are and to dust you shall return.' Dust is the symbol of coming to nothing: it has no content, no form, no shape; it blows away, the empty, indifferent, colourless, aimless, unstable booty of senseless change, to be found everywhere and at home nowhere. And scripture is right. We are dust. We are always in the process of dying. We are the only beings who know about this, know that we are bound for death, know that we are dust. Through our practical experience we come to realise that we are dust. Scripture tells us that we are like the grass in the field, like an empty puff of air. We are creatures of drifting perplexity. Despair is always threatening us and our optimism is a way of numbing bleak anxiety. Dust is what we are.

It is difficult for us to avoid hating ourselves. The reason why we cast our enemies down into the dust, tread them into dust, make them eat the dust, is because we are in despair about ourselves. What we cannot stand in others is what makes us despair about ourselves.

Dust has an inner relationship, if not an essential identity with the concept of 'flesh'. Flesh certainly designates in the Old and the New Testaments, the whole human person. It designates us precisely in our basic otherness to God, in our frailty, our weakness, our separation from God, which is manifested in sin and death. The two assertions, 'we are dust' and 'we are flesh' are, then, more or less essentially similar assertions.

But the good news of salvation rings out: 'The Word became flesh.' God himself has strewn his own head with the dust of the earth. He has fallen on his face upon the earth, which with evil greed drank up his tears and his blood. We can say to God exactly what is said to us: 'Remember that you are dust, and in death you shall return to dust.' We can tell him what he told us in Paradise, because he has become what we are after Paradise. He has become flesh, flesh that suffers even unto death, transitory, fleeting, unstable dust.

Ever since that moment, the sentence of terrifying judgement, 'dust you are,' is changed for people of faith and love. With the dust of the earth we trace on our foreheads the sign of the cross, so that what we are in reality can be made perceptible in a sign: people of death, people of redemption. 'Dust you are:' the judgement still has a myster- ious and shocking sense. The old sense is not abolished. But it descends with Christ into the dust of the earth, where it becomes an upward motion, an ascent above the highest heaven. 'Remember that you are dust:' in these words we are told everything that we are: nothingness that is filled with eternity; death that teems with life; futility that redeems; dust that is God's life forever.

From *The Eternal Year*, Burns & Oates, London, 1964. Used by kind permission of Continuum International Publishing Group Ltd.

Thursday after Ash Wednesday

Creeds, Christianity, Creation
James P. Mackey

Matthew, Mark and Luke place the story of the diabolical temptation of Jesus at the very beginning of his mission, enabling the author of the Epistle to the Hebrews to describe Jesus as 'one who in every respect has been tempted as we are, yet without sinning' (4:15). And since the story of that temptation is in the form of a myth, it must not be taken literally as something that happened only just after Jesus's baptism and before his public mission began. It must be taken as a temptation that is always waiting to surface in the forefront of his consciousness, as it regularly does to all of us, and as the text in Hebrews confirms. Indeed one can see specific evidences of that original temptation later in the story of Jesus's mission. For instance, he was tempted as a member of the Jewish people to see God as their God, when he was tempted to reject, and at first did reject the approach of a foreigner, and was saved by her faith from letting the temptation grow into a sin (Mt 15:21-28). And in the garden of Gethsemane he was tempted to refuse the bitter chalice of cruel execution that fidelity to the reign of the Creator God at that point required of him to drink to the very dregs (Mt 26:36-46). His closest disciples, and those who would be the leaders of the community of his followers, were not simply tempted but actually fell on important occasions. Peter, who at one moment was praised for his recognition of Jesus as the true messiah and son of

God, was certified satanic by Jesus at the very next moment
for refusing to contemplate the necessity of the cross for
the new life and witness of Jesus and his followers (Mt 16:
13-23).

From, *Christianity and Creation, The Essence of the Christian Faith
and its Future among Religions, A Systematic Theology,* Continuum,
New York & London, 2006, pp206-207. Used by kind permission
of Continuum International Publishing Group Ltd.

Friday after Ash Wednesday

The Meaning of the Great Fast
Kallistos Ware

If it is important not to overlook the physical requirements
of fasting, it is even more important not to overlook its
inward significance. Fasting is not a mere matter of diet. It
is moral as well as physical. True fasting is to be converted
in heart and will; it is to return to God, to come home like
the Prodigal to our Father's house. In the words of St John
Chrysostom, it means 'abstinence not only from food but
from sins.' 'The fast,' he insists, should be kept not by the
mouth alone but also by the eye, the ear, the feet, the hands
and all the members of the body.' It is useless to fast from
food, protests St Basil, and yet to indulge in cruel criticism
and slander: 'You do not eat meat, but you devour your
brother and sister.'

The inner significance of fasting is best summed up in
the triad: prayer, fasting, almsgiving. Divorced from prayer
and from the reception of the sacraments, unaccompanied
by acts of compassion, our fasting becomes pharisaical or
even demonic. It leads not to contrition and joyfulness, but
to pride, inward tension and irritability. Fasting is valueless
or even harmful when not combined with prayer. In the
gospels the devil is cast out, not by fasting alone, but by
'prayer and fasting'. These two should in their turn be
accompanied by almsgiving – by love for others expressed
in practical form, by works of compassion and forgiveness.
Without love towards others there can be no genuine fast.

This love should not be limited to formal gestures or senti-
mental feelings. It is to give not only our money but our
time, not only what we have but what we are; it is to give a
part of ourselves.

From *The Lenten Triodion*, Faber & Faber, London, 1978, pp 13-14.
Used by kind permission of the publisher.

Saturday after Ash Wednesday

The Meaning of the Great Fast
Kallistos Ware

The primary aim of fasting is to make us conscious of our
dependence upon God. If practised seriously, the Lenten
abstinence from food – particularly in the opening days –
involves a considerable measure of real hunger, and also a
feeling of tiredness and physical exhaustion. The purpose of
this is to lead us in turn to a sense of inward brokenness
and contrition; to bring us to the point where we appreciate
the full force of Christ's statement, 'Without Me you can
do nothing' (John 15:5). If we always take our fill of food
and drink, we easily grow over-confident in our own abilities,
acquiring a false sense of autonomy and self-sufficiency. The
observance of a physical fast undermines this sinful com-
placency. Lenten abstinence gives us the saving self-dis-
satisfaction of the Publican, making us 'poor in spirit,' aware
of our helplessness and of our dependence on God's aid.

Yet it would be misleading to speak only of this element
of weariness and hunger. Abstinence leads, not merely to
this, but also to a sense of lightness, wakefulness, freedom
and joy. Even if the fast proves debilitating at first, afterwards we find that it enables us to sleep less, to think more
clearly, and to work more decisively. As many doctors
acknowledge, periodical fasts contribute to bodily hygiene.
While involving genuine self-denial, fasting does not seek
to do violence to our body but rather to restore it to health
and equilibrium. Most of us in the Western world habitually
eat more than we need. Fasting liberates our body from the

burden of excessive weight and makes it a willing partner in the task of prayer, alert and responsive to the voice of the Spirit.

From *The Lenten Triodion*, Faber & Faber, London, 1978. Used by kind permission of the publisher.

First Sunday of Lent

Testing God's Son
Daniel J. Harrington

The customary title for this gospel is 'The Temptation of Jesus.' A better title, one more appropriate to the biblical basis of the narrative in the Book of Deuteronomy, is the 'Testing of God's Son.' The concern of the passage is not so much whether the devil can lure Jesus into this or that sin as it is the portrayal of Jesus as God's Son 'who in every respect has been tested as we are, yet without sin' (Heb 4:15). Where Israel in the wilderness failed, Jesus passes every test. After a narrative introduction, the Matthean version consists of three dialogues between the devil and Jesus and a narrative conclusion. Each dialogue has the devil offering a test and Jesus responding with a quotation from Deuteronomy 6–8. In these chapters Moses addresses the people of Israel near the end of their wanderings in the wilderness and before their entrance to the promised land.

Israel's experience in the wilderness is expressed in terms of a test from God: 'And you shall remember all the way which the Lord your God has led you these forty years in the wilderness, that he might humble you, testing you to know what was in your heart, whether you would keep his commandments or not' (Deut 8:2). Besides the testing motif this verse contains other themes developed by Matthew: Israel's being led by God, the number 40, the wilderness, the notion of fasting.

Whereas God may test Israel, Israel should not test God: 'You shall not put the Lord your God to the test, as you tested him at Massah' (Deut 6:16). Deuteronomy 6–8 not only supplies the three biblical quotations attributed to Jesus but also the key terms 'Son of God' and 'test'. Moses challenges Israel to learn from past mistakes in the wilderness and to act faithfully as they enter the Promised Land. Matthew presents Jesus as the true Son of God who passes the tests set forth by the devil and emerges as the model of covenant fidelity.

From *The Gospel of Matthew*, Sacra Pagina, Collegeville, MN: The Liturgical Press. Used by kind permission of the publisher.

Monday of the first week of Lent

Harden not your Heart
Eric Fromm

Freedom is not a constant attribute which we either 'have' or 'have not'. In fact, there is no such thing as 'freedom' except as a word and an abstract concept. There is only one reality: the act of freeing ourselves in the process of making choices. In this process the degree of our capacity to make choices varies with each act, with our practice of life. Each step in life which increases my self-confidence, my integrity, my courage, my conviction also increases my capacity to choose the desirable alternative, until eventually it becomes more difficult for me to choose the undesirable rather than the desirable action. On the other hand, each act of surrender and cowardice weakens me, opens the path for more acts of surrender, and eventually freedom is lost. Between the extreme when I can no longer do a wrong act and the other extreme when I have lost my freedom to right action, there are innumerable degrees of freedom of choice. In the practice of life the degree of freedom to choose is different at any given moment. If the degree of freedom to choose the good is great, it needs less effort to choose the good. If it is small, it takes a great effort, help from others, and favourable circumstances.

A classical example of this is the biblical story of Pharaoh's reaction to the demand to let the Hebrews go. He is afraid of the increasingly severe suffering brought upon him and his people; he promises to let the Hebrews go; but as soon as the imminent danger disappears, 'his heart hardens' and he again decides not to set the Hebrews free. The story of Pharaoh's hardening of heart is only the poetic expression of what we can observe every day if we look at our own development and that of others. The process of the hardening of the heart is the central issue in Pharaoh's conduct. The longer he refuses to choose the right, the harder his heart becomes. No amount of suffering changes this fatal development, and finally it ends in his and his people's destruction. He never underwent a change of heart, because he decided only on the basis of fear; and because of this lack of change, his heart became ever harder until there was no longer any freedom of choice left in him.

From *The Heart of Man*, Harper & Row, New York, 1968. Used by kind permission of HarperCollins, New York.

Tuesday of the first week of Lent

Moses and Pharaoh
Martin Buber

In the Egypt known from history the negotiations between the King and the representative of the slaves cannot possibly have assumed any such forms as those recorded; not even when the former accounts of the relations between that representative and the Court are given all due consideration. Further, the story of the plagues does actually link with natural phenomena of a kind that is, for the greater part, peculiar to Egypt. Yet how is it possible to enucleate an historical kernel from this breathless accumulation of extraordinary events, magnified immeasurably?

There are two recognised approaches in this regard: that of the person accepting traditions entire, holding that everything written here records something that has happened in fact in some specific place at some specific time; and that of the self-assured professional scholar who proposes to treat everything recorded here as literature pure and simple, and believes that it can be comprehended by literary categories. Between these two there is a third approach.

We must adopt the critical method and seek reality, here as well, by asking ourselves what human relation to real events this could have been which led gradually, along many bypaths and by way of many metamorphoses, from mouth to ear, from one memory to another, and from dream to dream, until it grew into the written account we have just read. It is certainly not a chronicle, but it is equally not imaginative poesy; it is an historical saga. As such it provides a starting point and a finishing-point. The starting-point is the return of Moses to Egypt. The finishing-point is the historically indisputable fact of the Exodus. What lies between these two? How did the Exodus come about, and what was Moses' share in it?

What is essential here can only be that historical situation which recurs again and again from Samuel to Jeremiah, the great refrain in Israel's history: prophet versus king. This historical phenomenon begins with Moses, and if his appearance before Pharaoh is regarded as the first in this series of prophetic incursions, there must remain a firm kernel of fact, after the dispersion of all the wonder-working which the Biblical account ascribes to Moses and his God. Disaster cannot indeed be directly induced, but it can be threatened, even though in general terms only, and such disasters as befall can be accounted for as an outcome of 'stiff-neckedness'. What is remarkable, yet still worthy of credence, is the fact that this process which mostly failed in later ages in the case of the kings of Israel, caused Pharaoh to fulfil the demand made of him.

From *Moses: The Revelation and the Covenant*, Harper Torchbooks, New York, 1958.

Wednesday of the first week of Lent

Israel in Egypt
Martin Buber

According to the biblical account the entry of the children of Israel into Egypt, and their departure 430 years later, were brought about by two Egyptianised Israelites. These had both been accepted in Pharaoh's court, one as Grand Vizier and the other as the adopted son of a princess; and both had received Egyptian names, one from a King, the other from a King's daughter. The narrative stresses the connection between the two when it relates how at the Exodus Moses himself brought forth the bones of Joseph, namely the mummy-coffin which is designated in the Hebrew text by a word bearing the meaning of a coffin nowhere else, but used for that Holy Ark which was the symbol of the covenant established between Yahweh and Israel by the words of Moses.

As far as our knowledge goes, Ancient Egypt was not merely the starting point of what we call civilisation; it was also the first, on such a scale at least, sole successful attempt to chill and congeal the life and spirit of humanity. That Egypt was a gift of the Nile can be fully appreciated only when the tremendous burden which this gift imposed upon those who settled in that country is realised. In order that the risen river might perform its fructifying work in adequate measure, without either harmful deficiency or even more harmful excess, the powers of nature had to be checked and regulated by a comprehensive system of dams, sluices, dykes and water-basins. Here, perhaps for the first time, human-

kind became familiar with the character of a perfectly organised duty of collective work. The taskmaster with the whip,
whom we meet in the biblical account of the slave-period of
Israel in Egypt is only a symbol of this collective duty, without which the very pyramids would never have come into
being. No less a symbol was the Pharaoh himself, who in his
own person, as it says in a pyramid text, incorporates 'the first
wave of the high water.' The perfect economic and political
centralisation which characterised Ancient Egypt has led
certain students to speak of it in terms of State socialism.

It would be incorrect to contrast this civilisation, based
as it is on the maintenance of fixed forms, with the Semitic
element as such. The factor, in the last resort antithetical
with Egypt comprehended only part of the Semites. This
factor is found in those hordes known as Habiri, whom we
find mentioned in numerous documents between the middle
of the third and the end of the second millennium BCE.

Habiru, or Hebrew, means not a tribe or a people but a
human type. They are people without a country, who have
dissociated themselves from their national connections and
unite in common journeys for pasture and plunder; semi-
nomadic herdsmen they are, or freebooters if opportunity
offers. What this type of life requires is a particular combination of the pastoral with the military virtues; but it also
calls for a peculiar mixture of adaptability and the urge to
independence. The civilisations into which they penetrate
are their opportunity; they are also their danger.

From *Moses: The Revelation and the Covenant*, Harper Torchbooks,
New York, 1958.

Thursday of the first week of Lent

The Passover
Martin Buber

Favourable circumstances have, within a relatively brief period, provided a man possessing the character and destiny of a leader with the external prerequisites for the fulfilment of his immediate task, the leading of a group of semi-nomadic tribes out of the land of 'bondage'. The geographical and political conditions under which the impending wandering has to take place are tremendously difficult, no matter whether that wandering already aims at landed possession and settlement or, for the time being, at the resumption of a nomadic life. The human groups whom he proposes to lead out are only loosely associated with each other; their traditions have grown faint, their customs degenerate, their religious association insecure. The great thought of the man, his great impulse, is to establish a covenant of the tribes in the purer and freer atmosphere of the desert, which had once purified and freed him himself. And so Moses reintroduces the holy and ancient shepherds' meal, renewed in meaning and form.

The essential thing to realise is that here a natural and customary human activity, that of eating, is elevated by the participation of the whole community to the level of an act of communion; and as such is consecrated to the God. It is eaten 'for him'. We do not know what the original meaning of the term *pessah*, translated Passover, may have been. The interpretation of the 'leaping over' the houses of Israel by Yahweh, the 'destroyer' during the night of the death of the first-born is, in any case, secondary; even though at the time of Isaiah this supplementary meaning had become established. The verb originally meant to move on one foot, to hop. It may be assumed that at the old nomad feast a hopping dance had been presented, possibly by boys masked as he-goats. Just as there are war dances in which the desired event is portrayed and simultaneously trained for until the mime suddenly becomes a reality, so, it may be imagined, a symbolic representation of the Exodus may have passed into the Exodus itself.

Moses transformed the clan feast of the shepherds (the unleavened flat cakes are the bread of the nomads) into the feast of a nation, without its losing its character of a family feast. And now the families as such are the bearers of the sacramental celebration; which, however, unites them into a national community. Moses did not change the custom of the ages into a cult; he did not add any specific sacrificial rite to it, and did not make it dependent on any sanctuary; but he consecrated it to Yahweh. He transformed the already existent Passover by introducing a new sense and symbol, as Jesus did later by the introduction of a new sense and symbol.

From *Moses: The Revelation and the Covenant*, Harper Torchbooks, New York, 1958.

Friday of the first week of Lent

Let My People Go
Martin Buber

Why does Pharaoh permit himself to be convinced? We find ourselves face to face with an historical mystery, one however which is historical and not literary in character. An historical mystery always means a relation between a super-personal fate and a person, and particularly that which is atypical in a person; that by which the person does not belong to his type. The task given to Moses is prophetic in character. But the fact that Moses fulfils it, tremendous as it is; that what has to be achieved is achieved; that unlike the later prophets of Israel he proves victorious in wrestling with the king; all this is clearly due to a large degree to the fact that he is something more than a prophet.

Though it may not be possible to determine what part of the 'plagues' belong to the kernel of truth and what is later crystallisation of legend, the four final plagues, as well as the second, retain a trace not only of actual events, but of events that belong to this period. Behind this passage stand both direct observation and an intention to describe the event as natural, and only its force as something unheard-of. The factual kernel of this we may assume to have been a plague which slew even the first-born son of Pharaoh. This is indicated by an assuredly early fragment which now stands shortly before the account of the Divine Attack: 'Thus said Yahweh, my first-born son is Israel. I said to thee, "Let my son go that he may serve me", but thou hast refused to let him go, so behold I slay thy first-born son.'

That is not a forecast of things to come, no demand or threat, but the words of the hour of destiny itself, suited precisely to the immediate moment breathing of inevitability. And the matter under consideration here lies not between Yahweh and Egypt, but between Yahweh and Pharaoh alone. Although the sonship of Israel implies not a mythical procreation but an historical act of adoption, it must be understood as a true state of sonship in order wholly to grasp the meaning of the words. It is one father speaking to another father.

And then, one spring, a sandstorm of hitherto unknown fury bursts out. The air is black for days on end. The sun becomes invisible. The darkness can be felt. All and sundry are paralysed and lose their senses. In the middle of this, however, while a pestilence, a children's epidemic, begins to rage and do its work, the voice of the mighty man sounds through the streets of the Royal City; unaffected by the driving masses of sand. The signs have persuaded his people. Massed around him, their hope is stronger than the darkness; they see light.

And then, after three days of the furious storm, the first-born son of the young king perishes in the night. Disconsolate in his innermost chamber, bowed over the little corpse, no longer a god but the very man that he is, he suddenly sees the hated one standing before him; and, 'Go forth!' he cries.

From *Moses: The Revelation and the Covenant*, Harper Torchbooks, New York, 1958.

Saturday of the first week of Lent

Saga and History
Martin Buber

In order to learn at first hand who Moses was and the kind of life that was his, it is obviously necessary to study the biblical narrative. There are no other sources worthy of serious consideration; comparison of reports, normally the chief means of ascertaining historical truth, is not possible here. Whatever has been preserved of Israel's traditions since ancient times is to be found in this one book. Not so much as the vestige of a chronicle dating from that period, or deriving from the nations with whom the children of Israel established contact on their journey from Egypt to Canaan, has been preserved; and not the vaguest indication of the event in question is to be found in ancient Egyptian literature.

The biblical narrative itself is basically different in character from all that we usually classify as serviceable historical sources. The happenings recorded there can never have come about, in the historical world as we know it, after the fashion in which they are described. The literary category within which our historical mode of thinking must classify this narrative is the saga; and a saga is generally assumed to be incapable of producing within us any conception of a factual sequence.

Further, it is customary to accept as a fundamental tenet of the non-dogmatic biblical scholarship of our day the view that the tales in question belong to a far later epoch than the events related, and that it is the spirit of that later epoch which finds expression in them; or, even more, the spirit of the sundry and various later periods to which are ascribed the 'sources'. Thus, Homer, for example, to take an analagous case, provides us with a picture of the epoch in which he himself lived rather than of the one in which his heroes did their deeds.

Assuming that to be the case, just as little could be ascertained regarding Moses' character and works as is to be ascertained of Ulysses. The scholarship of our own epoch, however, has prepared the way for another and deeper insight into the relation between saga or legend and history. The people of early times met the unplanned unexpected events which transformed the historical situation of their community at a single stroke with a fundamental stirring of all the elements in their being. It is a primeval state of amazement which sets all the creative forces of the soul to work. An organic and organically creative memory is here at work.

That this early saga, close as it is to the time of the event, tends to assume rhythmical form, can well be understood. What characterises this stage of human existence is that historical wonder can be grasped by no other form of speech save that which is rhythmically articulated, of course in oral expression. This is sustained by the wish to retain unchanged for all time the memory of the awe-inspiring things that had come about; to which end a transmission in rhythmical form is the most favourable condition.

From *Moses: The Revelation and the Covenant*, Harper Torchbooks, New York, 1958.

Second Sunday of Lent

The Transfiguration
Gregory Collins

One of the best ways to come close to Christ is to consider the gospel accounts of his transfiguration, which tradition says occurred on Mt Thabor. On the holy mountain shining in the full splendour of his glory, Jesus unveiled the deepest truth about himself before three of his apostles. But he also teaches us important things about ourselves as well.

First, Jesus takes the apostles away to be alone with him. The story of the transfiguration shows us that if we wish to focus properly on Christ, and come to the full knowledge of the truth about him, we must let him lead us into spaces filled with solitude. The apostles did not discern Christ's glory in the midst of the crowd, nor did they hear the Father's voice in the chaos and confusion of public ministry. 'If God would speak, you must be silent.'[1]

The second important thing revealed by the transfiguration is that one cannot remain permanently on the mountain-top, but must return to the chaos and confusion of the plain. Peter after all, had hoped to capture his transfiguring experience by building booths and remaining there, but it simply could not be. These eye-witnesses of the glory had to descend for, as Pope Saint Gregory the Great saw clearly, the life of the apostle entails a constant oscillation between the glorious vision in solitary prayer, and his struggle in service of the people.

---

1. John Tauler.

Finally, Maximos the Confessor suggests that when we take the Bible into solitude and listen attentively to the word of God, we are doing something similar to what the apostles did when they climbed the mountain with Jesus. By exposing our hearts to the word of scripture we may, by God's grace, catch a glimpse of his true Word, the incarnate Lord Jesus. For, the biblical words with their images and ideas are like the clothing of the Word. Just as Christ's clothes suddenly shone with the uncreated light of his divine glory, becoming dazzlingly white, so the words of the Bible may suddenly catch fire from the Word who clothes himself in them to speak to our hearts.

From *Come and Receive Light*, Columba, Dublin, 2003.

Monday of the second week of Lent

Crossing The Red Sea
Martin Buber

We do not know where the pursuers caught up with the fugitives, whether in the neighbourhood of the present Suez or further north at one of the bitter lakes or at the gulf of Akaba. Wherever it may have happened, however, there begins a natural process, or a series of natural processes (whether a combination of tides with unusual winds which raised them tremendously, or the effect of distant volcanic phenomena on the movement of the sea) which, together with a daring advance on the part of the Israelites and a destruction of the Egyptians, whose heavy war chariots are caught in the sand or the swamp, leads to the saving of the one and the downfall of the other.

What is decisive with respect to the inner history of humankind, however, is that the children of Israel understood this as an act of their God, as a 'miracle'; which does not mean that they interpreted it as a miracle, but that they experienced it as such, that as such they perceived it. This perception at the fateful hour, which is assuredly to be attributed largely to the personal influence of Moses, had a decisive influence on the coming into being of what is called 'Israel' in the religious history of humanity.

The concept of miracle which is permissable from the historical approach can be defined at its starting point as an abiding astonishment. The philosophising and the religious person both wonder at the phenomenon, but the one neutralizes this wonder in ideal knowledge, while the other abides in that wonder; no knowledge, no cognition can weaken this astonishment. Any causal explanation only deepens the wonder. The great turning-points in religious history are based on the fact that again and again and ever again an individual, and a group attached to that person, wonder and keep on wondering; at a natural phenomenon, at an historical event, or at both together; always at something which intervenes fatefully in the life of this individual and this group. They sense and experience it as a wonder. Miracle is not something 'supernatural' or 'superhistorical,' but an incident, an event which can be fully included in the objective, scientific nexus of nature and history; the vital meaning of which, however, for the person to whom it occurs, destroys the security of the whole nexus of knowledge, and explodes the fixity of the fields of experience named 'Nature' and 'History.' Miracle is simply what happens, in so far as it meets people who are capable of receiving it, or prepared to receive it, as miracle.

It is irrelevant whether 'much' or 'little,' unusual things or usual events happened; what is vital is only that what happened was experienced as the act of God.

The real miracle means that in the astonishing experience of the event the current system of cause and effect becomes transparent and permits a glimpse of the sphere in which a sole power, not restricted by any other, is at work. To live with the miracle means to recognise this power on every given occasion as the effecting one. That is the religion of Moses.

From *Moses: The Revelation and the Covenant*, Harper Torchbooks, New York, 1958.

Tuesday of the second week of Lent

Food for the Journey
Frances Hogan

The people had been told that they would see the glory of
God in the provision of manna, but what they actually
found the following day was a disappointment to them.
Whatever their imaginations had conjured up, the reality
was different. When the dew lifted from the desert they saw
'a thing delicate powdery as fine hoarfrost' on the ground,
and they said to one another: 'What is that?' 'That,' said
Moses, 'is the bread the Lord gives you to eat!' They were
puzzled and disappointed. They called it 'Man-hu' which
means 'What is that?' God never told them what it was,
except that this mysterious thing was to be their desert
food – their *viaticum* (food for the way) – until they reached
the Promised Land.

It was like coriander seed, white in colour, and resembled
wafers made with honey. Commentators say that manna
and the quails were a 'natural' event. Quails migrate across
the desert from North Africa to Southern Europe. Manna,
they say, is a secretion from insects which live in tamarisk
trees. This may be. But the manna recorded here has
mysterious properties. Even though some gathered more, and
some less, everyone had as much as they needed; if anyone
collected more than they needed for the day, it deteriorated
and bred maggots so it could not be used on the following
day. On the sixth day they could gather a double portion,
enough to last for the sabbath, and this portion did not
deteriorate or breed maggots; the manna ceased on the day

they set foot in the Promised Land (Joshua 5:12). It was eventually preserved successfully in a jar which was later put into the Ark of the Covenant with the tablets of stone, to remind the people of God's wonderful intervention on their behalf.

Manna typifies the spiritual nourishment essential for successful journeying through the wilderness. Jesus claims to be its fulfillment: 'I am the bread of life' (John 6:35). 'It was not Moses who gave you bread from heaven, it was my father, and this bread gives life to the world' (John 6:33). Manna remained a mystery to the pilgrims in the desert, but they took it, out of obedience to God. It was several hundred years later, with the full realisation of what manna really was, that they wrote in the Book of Wisdom (16: 20-21): 'You gave them the food of angels, from heaven untiringly sending them bread already prepared, containing every delight, satisfying every taste. And the substance you gave demonstrated your tenderness towards your children, for, conforming to the taste of whoever ate it, it transformed itself into what each eater wished.'

From *Words of Life from Exodus*, [Text abridged], Collins Fount, London, 1985, pp 144-54. Used by kind permission of the publisher.

Wednesday of the second week of Lent

Meribah
J. L. Mays

The story of the waters of Meribah tells of yet another
time when Israel, faced with the hardships of the wilderness,
turns on her leaders and questions her mission. But what is
of special concern in this story is that the failure of faith
reaches even to Moses himself, and as a result he and Aaron
join the generation of those who will not enter the
Promised Land. The people arrive at the wilderness of Zin,
the area to the north of the wilderness of Paran. The text
does not say in what year 'the first month' fell but it must
have been the fortieth year.

The lack of water incites the people to another rebellion.
As has become their custom in these uprisings, they heap
the entire responsibility for their predicament on the shoulders
of Moses, say they wish they were dead, and lamentingly
ask why they ever came out of Egypt to the hard barren
wilderness.

Moses and Aaron turn from the mob to the Lord, going
to the Tent of Meeting and falling on their faces. Knowing
in faith that this people is in the hands of the Lord, they
bear to him both the rebellion and the need of Israel.

The rock can only be the massive hill of solid rock from
beneath which the large spring of Kadesh still issues. Moses
is to assemble the congregation at the rock and, as they
look on, tell the rock to yield its water. The intention of so
arranging things is that the water should be more than a

mere drink to slake Israel's thirst; as their eyes saw the
Lord's provision for their need, the water would also revive
their fainting faith. In 1 Corinthians (10:4) Paul emphasises
this point. For him the rock represents Christ, and the
water is the spiritual gift which God supplies through his
Son for his people in their journey through life.

The act of bringing forth water was meant to hallow
the name of God and be a testimony to the people, but it
was not done so. Instead of speaking to the rock, Moses
struck it twice. Instead of pronouncing the word of the
Lord over the rock, Moses struck it, placing his own power
upon it, as magicians of the time would do. The people did
not hear the word of God, but saw Moses strike the rock.
On this occasion the frustration and anger of Moses
matched that of the people. Psalm 106 says that Israel
angered Moses and made his spirit bitter so that he spoke
rash words and it went ill with Moses on their account. The
waters are given the name Meribah, which in Hebrew
means 'contention.'

From *Leviticus, Numbers*, SCM Press, London, 1963. Used by kind
permission of the publisher.

Thursday of the second week of Lent

The Exodus
Walter Brueggemann

The narrative of the Exodus is designed to show the radical criticism and radical dismantling of the Egyptian empire. At the beginning the Egyptians are in full flower and full power. They 'wheel and deal' and are subject to none:

> Let heavier work be laid upon the men that they may labour at it and pay no regard to lying words. So the taskmasters and the foremen of the people went out and said to the people, 'Thus says Pharaoh ...' (5:7-10).

Notice how the language is shaped to evoke anger and bring to expression the deep resentment at this whole system. But the story moves. At the end, these same masters, taskmasters and foremen are vanquished, humiliated, and banished from history:

> The Egyptians whom you see today, you shall never see again (14:13).

From beginning to end the narrative shows, with no rush to conclude, how the religious claims of Egyptian gods are nullified by this Lord of freedom. The narrative shows with delighted lingering, how the politics of oppression is overcome by the practice of justice and compassion. And between the beginning and the end the moment of dismantling is the plague cycle, a narrative that cannot be told too often, for it testifies to what cannot be explained, surely not by the reason of the empire. It happens in this way: In the first two plagues, concerning the turn of the Nile and the frogs, the powerful work of Moses and Aaron is matched by Egyptian *techne*. Two plagues into the scene nothing is changed and the power of Egypt is not challenged. The empire knows how to play 'anything you can do, I can do better.' But then comes the third plague:

> Aaron stretched out his hand with his rod, and struck the dust of the earth, and there came gnats on man and beast; all the dust of the earth became gnats throughout all the land of Egypt. The magicians tried their secret arts to bring forth gnats, but they could not! (8:17-18)

The Egyptian empire could not! The gods of Egypt could not! The scientists of the regime could not. The imperial religion was dead! The politics of oppression had failed! That is the ultimate criticism, that the assured and alleged power of the dominant culture is now shown to be fraudulent. Criticism is not carping and denouncing. It is asserting that false claims to authority and power cannot keep their promises, which they could not in the face of the free God. It is only a matter of time until they are dead on the seashore.

From *The Prophetic Imagination*, Fortress Press, Philadelphia, 1982. Used by kind permission of Augsburg Fortress Publishers.

Friday of the second week of Lent

Mount Sinai
Martin Buber

When those who have grown up in the atmosphere of the
Bible think of the Revelation upon Sinai they immediately
see the mountain burning with fire up to the heart of the
heavens, darkness and cloud and lowering mist. And down
from above, down upon the quaking mountain, that smokes
like a furnace, descends another fire, flashing fire from heaven.
Various attempts have been made to refer this image back
to some natural event, either a tremendous thunderstorm or
the eruption of a volcano; but the singular wealth of
phenomena, which is inseparable from the description, runs
counter to such an explanation. What takes place here is a
meeting between two fires, the earthly and the heavenly;
and if either of them is struck out, there is an immediate
lacuna in the picture which has so enraptured the generations
of the people of Israel and the Christian peoples. Today,
however, something else is more important than all of this.
The spirit of our own times, which has grown mature and
more reserved, takes objection to the venerable image.
Moses who ascends the smoking mountain, who speaks to
the Height and receives from the thunder and trumpet-
blasts a response which he brings to the people in the form
of commandments and laws – that Moses is not merely a
stranger to us, he is unreal. The words of the Covenant, the
Ten Words, could surely not have entered the world in such
optical and acoustical pomp and circumstance; and where
the narrative reports them as having been written on

Tablets of Stone, things happen quite differently, in silence and solitude. We the late-born, oppressed as we are by the merciless problem of Truth, feel in our own minds a singular belated echoing of the protest which found its expression in the story of the Revelation to Elijah at Sinai. The voice comes not out of the storm, not out of the fury and the fire, but in a still, small whisper.

In any case every attempt to penetrate to some factual process which is concealed behind the awe-inspiring picture is quite in vain. We are no longer in a position to replace that immense image by actual data. It may be that one of those formidable thunderstorms, by which the Bedouins of this district are still struck with wonder from time to time as by a heavenly catastrophe, may have given the wandering people to know the primal force of the God who had been theirs from the times of the fathers, yet whom they now first 'came to know' in a nexus of actual events. Even if that is so, however, we can no longer substitute this for the traditional picture.

From *Moses: The Revelation and the Covenant*, Harper Torchbooks, New York, 1958.

Saturday of the second week of Lent

Decalogue?
Martin Buber

Why should there be a decalogue or anything resembling a decalogue? Why these ten commandments and no others? In order to find an answer we must first disabuse ourselves of the widely held view that the Decalogue is a 'catechism' which supplies the essence of the Israelite religion in a summary fashion, in articles of faith that can be counted on the ten fingers, and are specially prepared for learning by heart. If we have to think of ten fingers, then rather those of the law-giver himself, who was first a law-finder and who, so to say, sees in his two hands an image of the completeness requisite ere he raises those two hands towards the multitude. We miss the essential point if we understand the Decalogue to be 'the catechism of the Hebrews in the Mosaic period'. A catechism means an instruction for the person who has to be in a position to demonstrate their full membership of a religious community on the basis of general sentences which they recite either in complete or in abbreviated form. Such a catechism is correspondingly prepared partly in the third person as a series of statements, and partly in the first as a series of articles of personal faith.

The soul of the Decalogue, however, is to be found in the word 'Thou.' Here nothing is either stated or confessed; but orders are given to the one addressed, to the listener. In distinction to all catechisms and compositions resembling catechisms, everything here has reference to that specific hour in which the words were spoken and heard. It is possible that only the man who wrote down the words had once had the experience of feeling himself addressed; possibly he transmitted that which he heard to his people not orally, taking the 'I' of the god in his own mouth as though it were his own, but only in written form, preserving the necessary distance. At all times, in any case, only those persons really grasped the Decalogue who literally felt it as having been addressed to them themselves; only those, that is, who experienced that first one's state of being addressed as though they themselves were being addressed. Thanks to its 'thou,' the Decalogue means the preservation of the Divine Voice.

From *Moses: The Revelation and the Covenant*, Harper Torchbooks, New York, 1958.

Third Sunday of Lent

The Meaning of the Great Fast
Kallistos Ware

What is meant by the word 'fast'? Here the utmost care is
needed, so as to preserve a proper balance between the
outward and the inward. On the outward level fasting
involves physical abstinence from food and drink, and without
such exterior abstinence a full and true fast cannot be kept;
yet the rules about eating and drinking must never be treated
as an end in themselves, for ascetic fasting has always an
inward and unseen purpose. We are a unity of body and
soul, 'a living creature fashioned from natures visible and
invisible', and our ascetic fasting should involve both these
natures at once. The tendency to over-emphasise external
rules about food in a legalistic way, and the opposite tendency
to scorn these rules as outdated and unnecessary, are both
to be deplored.

The second tendency is doubtless the more prevalent in
our own day, especially in the West. Until the fourteenth
century, most Western Christians abstained during Lent not
only from meat but from animal products, such as eggs,
milk, butter and cheese. In East and West alike, the Lenten
fast involved a severe physical effort. But in Western
Christendom over the past five hundred years, the physical
requirements of fasting have been steadily reduced, until by
now they are little more than symbolic. How many, one
wonders, of those who eat panakes on Shrove Tuesday are

aware of the original reason for this custom – to use up any remaining eggs and butter before the Lenten fast begins?

If it is important not to overlook the physical requirements of fasting, it is even more important not to overlook its inward significance. Fasting is not a mere matter of diet. It is moral as well as physical. True fasting is to be converted in heart and will; it is to return to God, to come home like the Prodigal to our Father's house. In the words of St John Chrysostom, it means 'abstinence not only from food but from sins'. 'The fast,' he insists, should be kept not by the mouth alone but also by the eye, the ear, the feet, the hands and all the members of the body.' It is useless to fast from food, protests St Basil, and yet to indulge in cruel criticism and slander: 'You do not eat meat, but you devour your brother and sister.'

The inner significance of fasting is best summed up in the triad: prayer, fasting, almsgiving. Divorced from prayer and from the reception of the sacraments, unaccompanied by acts of compassion, our fasting becomes pharisaical or even demonic. It leads not to contrition and joyfulness, but to pride, inward tension and irritability. Fasting is valueless or even harmful when not combined with prayer. In the gospels the devil is cast out, not by fasting alone, but by 'prayer and fasting'. These two should in their turn be accompanied by almsgiving – by love for others expressed in practical form, by works of compassion and forgiveness. Without love towards others there can be no genuine fast.

From *The Lenten Triodion*, Faber & Faber, London. Used by kind permission of the publisher.

Monday of the third week of Lent

The Covenant
Martin Buber

The covenant entered into between the tribes and Yahweh contains in its very core the Covenant entered into between the tribes themselves; they became Israel only when they became partners in the Covenant of God.

We have good reason to assume that here we stand on historical ground. In our own days it has been convincingly demonstrated that the system of twelve tribes in Israel is not to be accounted for on the basis of natural growth, but is due to a regulation and division deriving from a specific historical situation. Nowadays there is a widely held view that no twelve tribes of Israel were ever in Egypt, that those who were in that country were the 'tribes of Joseph' and their followers, and that in Canaan these united for the first time into a complete twelve-tribe association. The presumed union is supposed to have taken place under Joshua's leadership at the 'Assembly in Shechem'. However, Joshua did not establish a new covenant but renewed the one which was in existence between Yahweh and Israel, just as it was repeatedly renewed during the ensuing period. He did this by re-establishing the Covenant, in accordance with the original intention of the founder, on the basis of an exclusive relationship with Yahveh and the elimination of all particularist idols. The *berith*, together with the system of the twelve tribes, was founded by Moses, and the evidence of the text just read does not need to be impugned. We do not know to be sure the names of the tribes referred to here, nor can we judge which of them were and which were not identical with those whose names have been preserved by tradition. But we may rest reasonably well assured that Moses, and none other than he, educed the tribal system of Israel. These tribes who have united in the Covenant with Yahweh are termed Israel as a collective unit. The interpretation of the name as meaning 'God rules' appears to have been an important factor. 'God Rules' is the proper name for the Holy Covenanters, which is what the tribes have become united for under Moses.

From *Moses: The Revelation and the Covenant*, Harper Torchbooks, New York, 1958.

Tuesday of the third week of Lent

The Young Bull
Martin Buber

The biblical narrative relates that while Moses remained on
the mountain to hear the injunction of God and to receive
the tablets from him, the people, despairing of his return,
demanded that Aaron should fashion them gods (*elohim*) to
go before them. They greet the image of a young bull made
by Aaron with the cry: 'These are your gods, O Israel, who
brought you up out of the land of Egypt.'

For the people who have to advance without any
knowledge of the way into the 'great and fearful wilderness',
the problem of guidance occupies the centre of their relations
to the God, which have been renewed for them through
the extraordinary man who has taken them in his charge.
He has brought them an assurance from this God, namely
that he wishes to lead and protect them; indeed, he has
taught them that such constant assistance, such a capacity
for remaining present, is an attribute of this Being and is
indicated in his name. But the constant and uniformly
functioning oracle to which they had looked forward has
not been provided for them. At their stations on the way
the extraordinary man used to wait for some kind of sign
or other, coming out of the mist or from somewhere else,
before he ordered them to commence their journey afresh.
They never knew what might happen at the next moment;
they could never depend on being able to rest next day in a
pleasant oasis in order to recover from the hardships of the
journey. He said, to be sure, did that man, that God goes

before them and that he makes his presence known by one sign or another sign; but the sole firm and unshakable fact was, in the last resort, that the God could not be seen; and all said and done you cannot actually follow something which you cannot see. All said and done, it is only the man who is followed, and they can all see how often he is uncertain, when he withdraws himself into his tent and broods for hours and days on end, until he finally comes forth and says that what has to be done shall be done in this and that way.

What kind of guidance is this, after all? And does it not mean that there must be something not quite in order between him and the God, if he cannot produce the God? He says, to be sure, that the God is not to be seen – but what can that mean? If you have a God, then to be sure you can naturally see him; you have an image and his strength is in that image. As long as you have no proper image you will have no proper guidance. And now, to cap it all, the man has vanished completely. He said that he is going aloft to the God up there, when we need the God down here just where we are; but he has not come back, and it must be supposed that that God of his has made away with him, since something or other between them was clearly not as it should have been. What are we to do now? We have to take matters into our own hands. An image has to be made, and then the power of God will enter the image and there will be proper guidance.

From *Moses: The Revelation and the Covenant*, Harper Torchbooks, New York, 1958.

Wednesday of the third week of Lent

The Tent of Meeting
Martin Buber

Once the catastrophe of the golden calf is at an end, what
had befallen overwhelms Moses even more than at the
moment of the first upgush of fury. Moses takes 'the tent',
his leader tent, which has hitherto stood in the midst of the
camp, and sets it 'for himself' outside the camp, where it
always has to be set thereafter at the stations of the way; but
no longer as a human leader's tent. He calls it the 'tent of
meeting' or 'the tent of coming together', and that is what
it has to be, no longer devoted to anything other than the
audiences granted him by his Lord. Henceforward he can
no longer enter the tent in the midst of the camp, as he had
presumably been accustomed to do; he can no longer seat
himself upon the ground and wait for that which we call
inspiration – an abstract word, which has become almost
too familiar, yet from which the original vivid sense of a
wafting-in of the divine breath has not yet passed away.

As before, Moses' own place remains in the camp of
'Israel'; there he belongs now as previously, but he can no
longer expect his God to come and visit him in a place that
has been polluted. If he wishes to question Yahweh thereafter,
he must leave the camp, he must go out to the tent that is
guarded by Joshua the most faithful one; and the people,
shaken and changed by that which has befallen them, rever-
ently watch him from time to time, each one standing at
the entry to their own tent. He does not prohibit any of
the people who wish to do so from coming to God about

any matter; they may approach the holy tent as they were wont to do, in order that counsel, instruction, decision might come to them from thence. But these are individuals; Yahweh no longer has any contact with the people as such.

That is the basic feeling of Moses after the catastrophe. But his feeling does not remain like that. It is rectified for him by a new experience of God.

Behind the ingeniously constructed conversations with God, we feel a reality that has been lived through. We have to regard it as a reality that Moses, after having been zealous for his zealous God, entreats him not to forsake the people whom he has brought hither 'upon eagles' wings', now that they have been unfaithful to the newly-concluded Covenant. And further it is an unmistakably genuine bio-graphical characteristic that while Moses is in 'the cleft of the rock', which the narrator assumes to be a familiar spot (near the place of the revelation at the Burning Bush), he, Moses, begs for the grace of the One who once addressed him from the flame, and is overwhelmed by a new experience of God. Moses had once learned two things in one at this spot: that Yahweh is present with his own, yet cannot be bound to any one fashion of manifestation. And likewise he now learns two things in one: of the graciousness and mercifulness of Yahweh, which are named as his essential attributes, and of his liberty to show these attributes to whomsoever he wishes to show them.

From *Moses: The Revelation and the Covenant*, Harper Torchbooks, New York, 1958.

Thursday of the third week of Lent

The Ten Commandments
Martin Buber

The story of the tables of the Ten Commandments as told
in the book of Exodus consists of a series of tremendous
scenes, which have always aroused the fervent emotions of
believing hearts. If we wish to keep before us a sequence of
events possible in our human world, we must renounce all
such tremendous scenes. Nothing remains for us except the
image, capable of being seen only in the barest outline and
shading, of the man who withdraws to the loneliness of
God's mountain in order, far from the people and over-
shadowed by God's cloud, to write God's law for the people.
To this end he has hewn *stelae* out of stone for himself. It
must be stone and not papyrus. For the hard stone is called
to testify, to serve as a witness. The stone outlasts the decaying
eyes and ears, and goes on speaking. In the same way
Moses, before the Covenant was made, had erected twelve
memorial stones for the twelve tribes which were to
become Israel at that hour.

Now, however, he goes further. There is one means of
placing a more comprehensive, clearer, verbally dependable
witness upon the stone. That is the wondrous means of
writing, which for early Israel was still surrounded by the
mystery of its origin, by the breath of God, who makes a
gift of it to us. By means of it one can embody in the stone
what has been revealed to one; so that it is no longer simply
an event, the making of the Covenant, but also, word by
word, it continues to serve as evidence of a revelation, of

the law of the King. What Moses says may be clumsy, but not what he writes: that is suitable for his time and for the later times in which the stone will testify.

And so he writes on the tables what has been introduced to his senses, in order that Israel may come about; and he writes it fittingly, as a finger of God. And the tables remain as tables of testimony or 'tables of making present', whose function is to make present unto the generations of Israel forever what had once become word; that is, to set it before them as something spoken to them in this very hour. And at an unknown hour the tables themselves pass out of our ken. The Word alone endures.

From *Moses: The Revelation and the Covenant*, Harper Torchbooks, New York, 1958.

Friday of the third week of Lent

The Ark
Martin Buber

The Royal Covenant is followed by the building of the throne. Moses and the representatives of Israel saw the footstool of the One who sat invisibly enthroned over the mountain, and it was 'a work of sapphire tiles'; now, out of the simple material available to him, he prepares a simply-joined Ark for Yahweh to rest his feet upon when he visits the people chosen by him in order to lead them in their wanderings and in battle. Over it, and possibly fashioned in the shape of yonder cloud-forms made radiant by the rising sun, rise the Cherubim, in order that their Lord should take his place to ride upon their horizontally-extended wings, which touch one another. Although the Ark has borrowed one or another motif from the heavenly vision of the elders, it does not in any way pretend to be a representation of the heavenly throne. In its purpose it is a meagre and necessarily dissimilar earthly substitute for it. And Yahweh who, when visiting his people, takes his seat upon it does so not as Cosmic King but as the Melek of Israel. The Babylonian divine thrones are nature symbols, that of Israel is a history symbol; and the tablets with the 'I' of God who has led the people out of Egypt are an inseparable part of it.

The foundation of this great Sacrum, like the foundation of all great symbols and sacraments in the history of religion, came about as the realisation of a paradox: an invisible God is sensed by the fact that he comes and goes, descends and rises. The view that Yahweh was imagined as residing above the Ark or actually in it misses the sense of this singular reality of faith. The effect of the Ark symbol was clearly so great that the movement of God was virtually sensed as a corporeal thing; so that the invisible God was himself apprehended. This is more than a continuous abiding; it is an ever-renewed coming, appearing, being present and accompanying. For the promise once developed from the name of God that he would 'be there' from time to time, and always at the moment when his presence was necessary, there is no more adequate material substratum to be thought of than this.

From *Moses: The Revelation and the Covenant*, Harper Torchbooks, New York, 1958.

Saturday of the third week of Lent

The Tabernacle
Martin Buber

The belief in the concentration from time to time of the
Divine Presence must, to be sure, have been transferred in
the popular mind to the Ark and the tent themselves; yet
every such 'coarsening of concept' can lead, through the
counter-movement of the spirit which it calls forth, to a
new deepening of the conception; a deepening which
admittedly also contains within itself the danger of abstraction;
that is, of a reduction in the awareness of vivid reality. The
hour of establishing a great symbol is apparently the only
one in which spirit and sensuous presentation maintain
their balance. Nevertheless, when Jeremiah or one of his
disciples, shortly after the Burning of the Temple, prophesies
a time at which the Ark of the Covenant will no longer be
remembered, since then the whole of Jerusalem will be
called the Throne of Yahweh, we should recognise this as
being a development of the original intention of the
foundation; for if the whole human world has become the
Kingdom of God, then Jerusalem as its midst should be his
throne, as once the Ark was Israel' wandering centre when
Yahweh became King of the people.

In Canaan the tent and the Ark appear to have been
long separated from one another, not only during the exile
of the Ark but also after its restoration through David, until,
as reported, they were both brought to the Temple under
Solomon, but were obviously not united. The Ark is placed
within the Holy of Holies; of the tent we hear nothing

more. However, we should not, with our historical comprehension of faith, regard as separated what was associated in the hour of foundation. The Ark, bearing the invisible and silent but effective Divine Presence, went ahead in the wanderings and campaigns; to the tent sheltering it at quiet times within the camp came the Presence, invisible as the voice which talks to Moses – in early texts out of the dark of the 'Pillar of Cloud,' and in later texts 'from between the two cherubim' – yet visible to the people as the radiation of the Divine substance, as the *kabod*; whether it be in the cloud lit up by the red of morning or in the sheet-lightning flashing incessantly near or far across the night sky; but always visibly directed towards or pointing to the tent.

It came to show and to warn, to arbitrate and to judge. Both of them, Ark and tent, belong to each other as the symbol of the double function of the Melek: that of leading his people through and defending them in an inimical world, and that of directing them through all the inner obstacles towards 'holiness'.

From *Moses: The Revelation and the Covenant*, Harper Torchbooks, New York, 1958.

Fourth Sunday of Lent

The Prophetic Imagination
Walter Brueggemann

The task of prophetic imagination and ministry is to bring
to public expression those very hopes and yearnings that
have been denied so long and suppressed so deeply that we
no longer know they are there. Hope, on the one hand, is
an absurdity too embarrassing to speak about, for it flies in
the face of all those claims we have been told are facts.
Hope is the refusal to accept the reading of reality which is
the majority opinion, and one does that only at great political
and existential risk. On the other hand, hope is subversive,
for it limits the grandiose pretension of the present, daring
to announce that the present to which we have all made
commitments is now called into question.

Speech about hope cannot be explanatory and scientifically
argumentative; rather, it must be lyrical in the sense that it
touches the hopeless person at many different points. More
than that, however, speech about hope must be primally
theological, which is to say that it must be in the language
of covenant between a personal God and a community.
Promise belongs to the world of trusting speech and faithful
listening. It will not be reduced to the 'cool' language of
philosophy or the private discourse of psychology. It will
finally be about God and us, about his faithfulness that
vetoes our faithlessness. Hope is the decision to which God
invites Israel, a decision against despair, against permanent
consignment to chaos, oppression, barrenness, and exile.

Hope is the primary prophetic idiom not because of the

general dynamic of history or because of the signs of the times but because the prophet speaks to a people who are God's people. Hope is what this community must do because it is God's community.

Of course prophetic hope easily lends itself to distortion. It can be made so grandiose that it does not touch reality; it can be trivialised so that it makes no impact on reality; it can be 'bread and circuses' only supporting and abetting the general despair. But a prophet has another purpose in bringing hope to public expression, and that is to return the community to its single referent, the sovereign faithfulness of God. It is only that return which enables a rejection of the closed world of royal definition. Only a move from a managed world to a world of spoken and heard faithfulness permits hope. It is that overriding focus which places Israel in a new situation and which reshapes exile, not as an eternal fate but as the place where hope can most amazingly appear. There is no objective norm that can prevent a prophet of hope from being too grandiose or too trivial. It is likely that the only measure of faithfulness is that hope always comes after grief and that the speaker of this public expression must know and be a part of the anguish which permits hope. Hope expressed without knowledge of and participation in grief is likely to be false hope that does not reach despair.

From *The Prophetic Imagination*, Fortress Press, Philadelphia, 1982. Used by kind permission of Augsburg Fortress Publishers.

Monday of the fourth week of Lent

The Idea of a Scapegoat
James Danaher

The ancient Hebrews needed some way to feel that they were worthy to come into the presence of a holy God. Their all-too-human idea was that the greatness of God precluded God from loving or even tolerating anything that was not perfect. Such a notion kept them at a distance from God. If they were to approach God, they would have to feel that they were somehow good in God's sight. But they knew of their own imperfection. Thus, a scapegoat, upon whom they could put all of their sin and guilt, was necessary in order for them to come into God's presence, but it was not necessary for God. For many of us, Jesus is the scapegoat who allows us to approach a God who we think is otherwise unapproachable.

Certainly no one comes to God except through the atoning work of Jesus, but if we need, because of our understanding, to believe that Jesus is our scapegoat who allows us to enter into a relationship with God, the scripture miraculously allows for such an understanding. Equally, it allows us to see atonement as a matter of ransom or forgiveness if that is what our understanding requires.

For many, the idea of a scapegoat provides a means that allows human beings to cross over and enter into a relation-ship with God. It is not, however, a means which God requires in order to cross over and enter a relationship with human beings. Since God can maintain a relationship with human beings through pure forgiveness, Jesus may be our scapegoat but he is not God's scapegoat. What separates us from God is not God's sense of justice but our sense of justice. Jesus is our scapegoat and bears our sin, not to appease God, but to appease our understanding so we might no longer fear God's presence.

God's desire has always been that we would enter into relationship with God, but our all-too-human concepts and our idea of who God is, have kept us from that relationship. We imagine that God is like us and can only love that which is beautiful and good, but God is not like us. God can love the unlovely. God even loves God's enemies. Unlike human beings who are for the most part incapable of forgiveness and demand payment for an offence by the guilty, God is capable of forgiveness through which God makes payment in order to restore relationship with us. Since this is unfathomable to most of us, God gave the scapegoat as a means for humans to approach the Godhead. It is the entering into relationship with God that is important and not a correct theology about how that happens. If we are not capable of a correct understanding, God in God's mercy gives us an understanding we can grasp.

From 'A Contemporary Perspective on Atonement', *Irish Theological Quarterly*, 69 (2004) No 3. Used with permission from the editor, by permission of Sage Publications Ltd.

Tuesday of the fourth week of Lent

Love your neighbour
Martin Buber

There are four things above all which have to be protected
in order that the community may stand firm in itself: life,
marriage, property and social honour. The damaging of
these four basic goods and basic rights of personal existence
is forbidden in the most simple and pregnant formulas. But
these are not enough to protect the community from dis-
organisation, on account of all the kinds of inner conflicts
which might break out. They apply only to actions, to the
active outcome of passions or feelings of ill-will directed
against the personal sphere of other people; they do not
involve attitudes which have not passed into action.

There is one attitude which destroys the inner connection
of the community even when it does not transform itself
into actual action; and which indeed, precisely on account
of its passive or semi-passive persistence, may become a
consuming disease of a special kind in the body politic. This
is the attitude of envy. The prohibition of 'covetousness' is
to be understood as a prohibition of envy. The point here is
not merely a feeling of the heart but an attitude of one
person to another which leads to a decomposition of the
very tissue of society.

In a community which was being broken up from
within by a vast increase of social inequality, by the misuse
of the power of property in order to gain possession of
smaller properties, by the exploitation of the strength of the
economically weaker and dependent; in a community

wherein, generation after generation, rang the great protests of the prophets, no central and authoritative collection of the laws indispensable for the inner strengthening of the community could have been thinkable which did not expressly combat social injustice. It is appropriate to a period in which, to be sure, inequalty of property is already to be found; but in which, taking the whole situation into account, that inequality does not yet lead to any fateful misuses, so that the immediately obvious danger deriving from it is envy and not oppression.

From *Moses: The Revelation and the Covenant*, Harper Torchbooks, New York, 1958.

Wednesday of the fourth week of Lent

The Spirit
Martin Buber

A clear distinction is drawn in respect of the gifts of the
spirit. The *ruah* 'is' over Moses; on the 'Seventy' it comes to
rest, leads to extraordinary but temporary behaviour on
their part; and the fact that they have once experienced this
condition, this stirring up and perception of all the forces,
thereafter enables them to help Moses in 'bearing' the people.
Moses himself does not require to undergo any such
process; he to whom the Voice has spoken, as one person to
another, has become the carrier of the Spirit, of a resting
and constant spirit without any violent effects; a spirit
which is nothing other than an assumption into a dialogic
relationship with the Divinity, into the colloquy. As against
this, the *ruah* which takes possession of the elders is an
impersonal, wordless force. The spiritual experience of the
elders corresponds to the workings of the *ruah* in the period
following the conquest of Palestine, from the first great
'Judges' until the commencement of the kingdom; and
which is found with the most clarity in the case of Saul.
On one single occasion the spirit descends upon the charismatic one and turns him into 'another man,' endowing him
with special powers for his office.

Moses appears as raised above the 'Judges' and their
spiritual experience; for mission is greater than induction
into office, even that of a commander in a war of liberation,
as in the cases of the Judges and of Saul. The mission takes

place above the sphere of the impersonal *ruah*; it takes place in the sphere of the Word.

As the emissary of Yahweh Moses is contrasted with and elevated above the elders. But the narrator does not wish this superiority to be understood as something desired by Moses himself, who was 'very humble,' but as the fate with which he has been charged by God and which oppresses him. He tells the episode of the two men who remained amid the tents of the camp instead of 'going forth' to the Tent of Meeting, which stood in the middle of the circle, and who were possessed by the Spirit where they stood. Joshua wishes the latter to 'withhold' the presumptuous fellows. Moses, however, disapproves of his 'zeal' on his behalf; if only, says he, the whole people were prophets! By saying this Moses only reiterates the hope that at some time the Spirit might be shared by all. For when the whole people have become prophets, in direct contact with God, it will no longer be necessary for somebody to be charged by God with the function of bearing them on his bosom like an infant.

From *Moses: The Revelation and the Covenant*, Harper Torchbooks, New York, 1958.

Thursday of the fourth week of Lent

The Land
Martin Buber

According to the account in the Book of Numbers, Moses
sends spies from Kadesh to Canaan. They bring back good
and bad tidings. Shaken by the unfavourable part of the
reports, the people lament, speak of appointing themselves a
new head and returning to Egypt; those who offer them
opposition are in danger of being stoned. At this point
Yahweh intervenes; he wishes to destroy the people , and to
let the offspring of Moses serve for the making of a fresh
one. Moses intercedes and wins foregiveness for them, but
the sinful generation is condemned to perish in the wilderness; forty years must pass before Israel enters Canaan.

Kadesh should not be understood as meaning a single
spot, but the entire group of level valleys lying south of
Palestine on the way between Akaba and Beersheba, which
link up with the place of that name; valleys surrounded by
hills, where springs gush forth, so that sometimes the water
bursts from the clefts and crannies of the rocks. The land is
rich in water and fruitful for the greater part; here and
there, indeed, of a paradisical fruitfulness. To this day the
soil, which is several feet deep, still provides the Arabs who
till it with rich harvests of grain when there has been a
good rainy season. The district has noteworthy remains of
Syro-Canaanite culture, dating from the second half of the
second millennium BCE, including a fortress which is
supposed to have been already standing when Moses and
his hosts came there; and the presence of which makes it

possible to explain the biblical description of Kadesh as a
'town' or fortified place.

The people may have fixed on this spot, which was so
suitable for the purpose, as the centre of their movements;
where Moses remained with the Ark and the armed Levite
guard, while the tribes swarmed forth. The fruitful soil was
tilled, as already had been done by the 'Fathers,' with primitive
but productive methods; and the herds were driven to pasture
in the neighbourhood. The Hebrews had returned not only
'to the place of the Fathers' but also to their form of life.

But is the urge to Canaan to be attributed to the fact
that the rapid increase of the people made it necessary to
find more room? Or was Kadesh regarded from the very
beginning as no more than a station, the prolonged
sojourning in which was an outcome of the historical
circumstances? Is the promise to Moses of a 'good broad
land' to be explained as due to a later shaping of the
Exodus tradition, or ought we to understand it as an essential
motive in Moses' own actions? When Moses departed from
Egypt, did he wish only to liberate the tribes? Or did he
wish to lead them to settle as well? Was the memory of the
Canaan of the Fathers at work in him as a hope and
aspiration? In the religious field he had sought and found,
in a passionately remembered past, the basis of the future
which he wished to build. Was this equally true in the field
of actual history?

From *Moses: The Revelation and the Covenant*, Harper Torchbooks,
New York, 1958.

Friday of the fourth week of Lent

The Promised Land
Martin Buber

In our own times critical investigation is once again beginning to recognise that the elements of the promising of the land in the legends of the fathers is not in itself a free creation of the Yahwist, a predating, perchance, of the needs of the tradition of the occupation of the land, but belongs to old and indeed to the oldest traditions. It will not do to view the stories of the Fathers as no more than a pseudo-historical justification of the claim to Canaan. The fathers owed their position in the Israelite traditional sagas primarily to their function as recipients of revelation, and at the same time to the relations of the divinities revealing themselves to them to genealogically confirmed associations, to clans and tribes, as well as to the fact that this type of religion contained within itself a tendency to the social and the historical, which corresponds to the conditions of life in nomadic tribes.

As far as can be judged, the tribes in Egypt were restricted to cattle-raising, and the period of forced labour is scarcely likely to have served them as preparation for agriculture; neither in Midian nor afterwards in Egypt could Moses ever have come to realise all the external and internal transformations that were bound to be involved in a transfer to a predominantly agrarian form of life. This can only have begun to become clear to him at Kadesh, with the beginning of the people's experience in some measure of tilling the soil.

Kadesh means 'sanctuary'; since ancient times it has been called 'Fountain of Judgement'; it was a holy well. As the thought of the land became more concrete, Moses would also have begun to consider the necessity of legal provisions such as might serve to regulate the new form of life in a fashion that could secure the conditions of a just social life, which he may well have known from nomadic tribal traditions and his own experience with the people, against grave disturbance. And here he would have had to start out from his basic idea, that of the real and direct rule of God; which would necessarily have led to the postulate that God owns all the land.

From *Moses: The Revelation and the Covenant*, Harper Torchbooks, New York, 1958.

Saturday of the fourth week of Lent

The Bronze Serpent
Marcia Montenegro

The significance of looking on the bronze serpent and living is that the healing is based on faith, not on the copper serpent itself.

In the Exodus confrontation between Moses and Pharaoh, Aaron's serpent is a duplication of the legendary magicians' power of turning a staff into a serpent, but it is also more than a duplication. When Aaron's serpent swallows the magicians' serpents, it is God trumping Pharaoh at his own game, both realistically and metaphorically, since the cobra is a symbol of power in Egypt and its figure decorates the crowns of both Pharaoh and sun god Ra. The serpent is used as an instrument of God's power. Rather than show His power in a way divorced from their culture, Yahweh challenges Pharaoh using the very elements of Egyptian beliefs in serpents and magic to turn the situation around to his advantage.

If 'fiery' in this passage refers to the serpents' deadly venom, then God is telling Moses to make a bronze model of a poisonous snake. Thus, the replica of the very source of poison and death becomes the symbol and means of healing, but the healing is by faith, not magic. Yahweh has no need for magic, as do the gods of Egypt. The bronze serpent has no powers in itself; it is God who heals, but the people must individually look in faith to that bronze serpent to receive the healing. This episode became the basis for Jesus' statement in John 3:14, 15, that as the serpent in the wilderness was lifted up, so must he be lifted up, that all who believe in him shall have eternal life. In both cases, the means of death becomes the means of life.

Just as the New Testament has both good and bad references to serpents (Jesus telling the disciples to be 'wise as serpents', in Matthew 10:16; the allusion to the bronze serpent in John 3:14; Jesus rebuking the Pharisees as serpents and vipers in Matthew 23:33; and Satan identified as the dragon in Revelation, chapter 12), so does the Pentateuch present the serpent as both good and evil.

In the Pentateuch, the serpent is a multi-faceted metaphor and symbol. It does not have a rigid, static meaning, as it is not always used to represent the same thing. The serpent is, after all, a creature created by God. Just as Satan used the serpent for his purposes in the Garden, so did God use the serpent to reproach Pharaoh and to show his power over Egypt, and for the healing of his people in the wilderness. One can discern a progression, not necessarily intended, of the serpent in these passages, going from evil in the Garden, to ambiguous in the blessing of Dan, to a more neutral but compelling tool of God's power in Pharaoh's court, and finally becoming a symbol or instrument of healing in the wilderness, an image later used by Christ himself to illustrate his saving power over death. The deadly serpent is transformed into an icon of healing and life, just as the death that came in the Garden was overcome by the gift of eternal life offered through Christ's atonement on the cross.

Fifth Sunday of Lent

The Meaning of the Great Fast
Kallistos Ware

'We waited, and at last our expectations were fulfilled,' writes the Serbian Bishop Nikolai of Ochrid, describing the Easter service at Jerusalem. 'When the Patriarch sang "Christ is risen", a heavy burden fell from our souls. We felt as if we also had been raised from the dead. All at once, from all around, the same cry resounded like the noise of many waters. "Christ is risen", sang the Greeks, the Russians, the Arabs, the Serbs, the Copts, the Armenians, the Ethiopians – one after another, each in their own tongue, in their own melody … Coming out from the service at dawn, we began to regard everything in the light of the glory of Christ's Resurrection, and all appeared different from what it had yesterday; everything seemed better, more expressive, more glorious. Only in the light of the Resurrection does life receive meaning.'

The season of Lent falls not in midwinter when the countryside is frozen and dead, but in the spring when all things are returning to life. The English word 'Lent' originally had the meaning 'springtime,' the lengthening of days. Lent signifies not winter but spring, not darkness but light, not death but renewed vitality. It is a time not of gloom but of joyfulness. It is true that fasting brings us to repentance and to grief for sin, but this penitent grief, in the vivid phrase of St John Climacus, is a 'joy-creating sorrow'.

Our fasting should not be self-willed but obedient. When we fast, we should not try to invent special rules for ourselves, but we should follow the accepted pattern, expressing as it does the collective conscience of the People of God, possesses a hidden wisdom and balance not to be found in ingenious austerities devised by our own fantasy. If proud and wilful, our fasting assumes a diabolical character, bringing us closer not to God but to Satan. Because fasting renders us sensitive to the realities of the spiritual world, it can be dangerously ambivalent: for there are evil spirits as well as good.

A sense of resurrection joy is the foundation of all our Christian worship; it is the one and only basis for our life and our hope. Yet, in order for us to experience the full power of this Paschal rejoicing, each of us needs to pass through a time of preparation. 'We waited,' says the bishop, 'and at last our expectations were fulfilled.' Without this waiting, without this expectant preparation, the deeper meaning of the Easter celebration will be lost.

So it is that before the festival of Easter there has developed a long preparatory season of repentance and fasting. Balancing these weeks of Lent and Holy Week, there follows after Easter a corresponding season of thanksgiving, concluding with Pentecost.

Just as the children of Israel ate the 'bread of affliction' in preparation for the Passover, so Christians prepare themselves for the celebration of the New Passover by observing a fast.

From *The Lenten Triodion*, Faber & Faber, London, 1978. Used by kind permission of the publisher.

Monday of the fifth week of Lent

Epistle to the Hebrews
Raymond E. Brown

By all standards this is one of the most impressive works in the New Testament. Consciously rhetorical, carefully constructed, ably written in quality Greek, and passionately appreciative of Christ, Hebrews offers an exceptional number of unforgettable insights that have shaped subsequent Christianity.

Yet in other ways it is a conundrum. It tells us virtually nothing about the author, the locale, the circumstances or the addressees. Almost all our information pertinent to the background of the text must come from an analysis of the argumentation advanced by the author. Early commentators on this work saw 'the literary riddle of the Epistle to the Hebrews' in its beginning like a treatise, proceeding like a sermon and closing like an epistle.

Some refer to Hebrews as pseudonymous; but 'anonymous' is more accurate since no claim is made within the work about its writer. Yet by the end of the second century some were attributing it to Paul. Gradually the name of Paul was introduced into the title of the work, appearing both in the Vulgate (and English translations drawn from it) and the King James Version. Nevertheless, the evidence against Paul's having written it is overwhelming. The elaborate, studied Greek style is very different from Paul's, as Clement and Origen already recognised.

We have to be satisfied with the irony that the most sophisticated rhetorician and elegant theologian of the

New Testament is an unknown. To employ his own description of Melchisedek, the writer of the epistle to the Hebrews remains without father or mother or genealogy.

From *An Introduction to the New Testament*, Yale University Press, 1997. Used by kind permission of the publisher.

Tuesday of the fifth week of Lent

Epistle to the Hebrews
Raymond E. Brown

The high priesthood of Jesus Christ is a major theme of the
epistle to the Hebrews. To some extent this is a surprise
since the historical Jesus was emphatically a layman, critical
to some degree of Temple procedure and treated with
hostility by the Temple priesthood. The solution of
Hebrews that his was a priesthood according to the order
of Melchizedek may be original, but the idea of Jesus'
priesthood is found in other New Testament works chiefly
in relation to his death. In particular, John (10:36; 17:19)
uses the verb 'consecrate, make holy' used by Exodus
(28:41) for Moses' consecration of priests. After reflecting
on the text, one may ask how the appropriation of Israelite
liturgical language (Tabernacle, Temple, priesthood, sacrifices,
feasts) for Jesus affects the use of that language for later
Christians. The attitude has not always been consistent.
Many have no objection to the description of Holy
Thursday/Easter as a Christian Passover. Yet they may reject
vigorously the terminology of sacrifice and priest in
Christian cult. In loyalty to the once-for-all outlook of
Hebrews, churches that do use sacrificial terminology stress
that the eucharist is no new sacrifice but the liturgical
making-present of the sacrifice of Christ. Although Clement
juxtaposed the Jewish high priest, priest, and levite to
Christ, the bishop, and the deacon, the first clear use of
'priest' for the principal Christian eucharistic minister (the
bishop) comes at the end of the second century. By the

fourth century all eucharistic ministers were considered to be Christian priests, sharing in Christ's priesthood according to the order of Melchisedek.

From *An Introduction to the New Testament*, Yale University Press, 1997. Used by kind permission of the publisher.

Wednesday of the fifth week of Lent

The Priest as Poet of the Word
Karl Rahner

There are words which divide and words which unite:
words which can be artificially manufactured and arbitrarily
determined and words which have always existed or are
newly born as by a miracle; words which unravel the whole
in order to explain the part, and words which by a kind of
enchantment produce in the person who listens to them
what they are expressing. They are like sea-shells, in which
can be heard the sound of the ocean of infinity, no matter
how small they are in themselves. They bring light to us,
not we to them. They have power over us, because they are
gifts of God, not our own creations, even though they may
have come through other human beings to us. Some words
are clear because they are shallow and without mystery;
they suffice for the mind; by means of them one acquires
mastery over things. Other words are obscure because they
evoke the blinding mystery of things. Such words, which
spring up out of the heart, which hold us in their power, I
would like to call primordial words, as opposed to the other
kind which are fabricated, technical, utility words.

Primordial words are always filled with the soft music of
infinity. No matter what they speak about, they always
whisper something about everything. They are the children
of God, who possess something of the luminous darkness of
their Father.

It is to the poet that the word has been entrusted. The
poet is capable of speaking the primordial words in powerful

concentration. Everyone pronounces primordial words. Everyone calls things by their names and so continues the action of their father Adam. But the poet has the calling and the gift of speaking such words in powerful concentration. The poet has the power to speak them in such a way that, by means of this word, things move as though set free into the light of others who hear the words of the poet.

Is the priest then simply the poet? This cannot be answered with a simple 'yes'. For the priest is so much more than the poet. We would be saying too little if we were to call the priest simply the poet of the word of God. Too little, because each one possesses their own proper name which is irreducible and cannot be replaced by any other word. Their name is: priest. Priests may communicate their message without concern. Perhaps it is on their lips without having proceeded from their heart. Perhaps their life does not make a reality of what they are saying. Nevertheless, they remain a priest, herald of the word of God in virtue of a holy mission. But one could not then call them a poet any more. For one can be a poet only if the word of the mouth springs up from the centre of the heart. One can say the words of God without expressing oneself.

The word of God in the mouth of the priest wants, if it is to be spoken rightly, to absorb the life of the priestly individual. It calls upon the whole person and lays claim to everything that person is and does.

From *Theological Investigations*, Vol III, Datron, Longman and Todd. Used by kind permission of the publisher.

Thursday of the fifth week of Lent

The Priesthood of the Pagans
Sergius Bulgakov

In the Hebrew Testament, the Holy Spirit inspired
Melchisedek, pagan priest, to seek out and bless Abraham.
And this same Melchisedek is representative of the ever-
present priesthood of the so-called 'Pagans'. Even before
the levitical priesthood was established, this priest from
nowhere was anointed by the Holy Spirit. His pneumatic
priesthood is invoked in Psalm 109 as guarantor of all others:
'A prince from the day of your birth on the holy mountains;
from the womb before the dawn I begot you. The Lord has
sworn an oath he will not change: "You are a priest forever,
a priest like Melchisedek of old".'

We must recognise and value the legitimate piety of
non-Christian peoples, manifested in their seeking God,
their prayer, their sacrifices and good works, because 'God
makes no exceptions of persons; anyone from any nation
who fears God and acts justly is agreeable to God' (Acts
10:34-35). What is said of Cornelius in the Acts of the
Apostles applies to all pagan piety, which in spite of an
inevitable and inexorable opacity, carries with it the blessing
of God.

The Epistle to the Hebrews devotes a whole chapter to
explaining that Jesus Christ is in fact a second Melchisedek,
'who is a priest not by virtue of a law about physical
descent, but by the power of an indestructible life.' This
indestructible life is the Holy Spirit in person. And the
pagan priest anointed by that same Spirit is invoked even in

the Canon of the Roman Catholic Mass: 'Look with favour on these offerings and accept them as once you accepted the sacrifice of your servant Abel, the sacrifice of Abraham, our father in faith, and the bread and wine offered by your priest, Melchisedech.' We cannot but gaze in wonder at the portrait of this priest-king Melchizedek emerging from the darkness of paganism to bless Abraham and offer him gifts of bread and wine prefiguring the eucharist. In the meeting of Abraham with Melchizedek we see an encounter, through the Holy Spirit, of two equally valid priesthoods, one inside the church, one outside (Genesis: 14:18-20).

From *Le Paraclet*, Éditions l'Age d'Homme, Paris, 1996. Used by kind permission of the publisher.

Friday of the fifth week of Lent

Eternal Sacrifice
Raymond E. Brown

The main contrast is between two divine revelations: one by the prophets and the other by a preexistent Son through whom God created the world and who has now spoken to us. The description, in language that may be drawn from a hymn, shows that the writer is interpreting Christ against the background of the Old Testament portrayal of divine Wisdom. Just as Wisdom is the effusion of God's glory, the spotless mirror of God's power who can do all things, God's Son is the reflection of God's glory and the imprint of God's being, upholding the universe by his word of power. Going beyond the Wisdom pattern, however, the Son is a real person who made purification for sins, and that accomplishment is intimately related to the Son taking his seat at the right of the Majesty.

This extraordinarily 'high' christology is now worked out in the Son's superiority over the angels and over Moses. The whole of Chapter Seven is devoted to the superiority of the priesthood possessed by Jesus over the levitical priesthood. Several points constitute the superiority of Melchisedek: He blessed Abraham; his priesthood was accompanied by the Lord's oath; and above all a priest according to the order of Melchisedek is eternal. There is no longer a need for numerous (levitical) priests who are replaced after death because Jesus who has the Melchisedek priesthood continues forever, making intercession. When he offered himself, this holy, blameless, undefiled high priest, separated from sinners and exalted above the heavens, effected a sacrifice which is once for all.

From *An Introduction to the New Testament*, Yale University Press, 1997. Used by kind permission of the publisher.

Saturday of the fifth week of Lent

The Day of the Lord
Alexander Schmemann

For an understanding of the place of the 'Lord's Day' in the liturgical life of the early church it is important to clarify its relationship to the Hebrew sabbath. Christian thought has so ignored this relationship that the whole week has been simply 'advanced,' and the day of resurrection (the first day of the week, the *prima sabbati*) has gradually become another sabbath. All the Old Testament prescriptions and definitions touching the seventh day were little by little transferred to Sunday, and the seventh day has been converted into a kind of 'prototype' of the Christian day of rest. This displacement of the week became especially apparent when the emperor Constantine gave the 'day of the sun' an official state sanction, and made it a generally obligatory day of rest. But even before the end of the fourth century, the memory still lived in the mind of the church of the original relationship of the 'Lord's Day' with the sabbath and the whole Old Testament week.

For the early church the Lord's Day was not a substitute for the sabbath; it was not (so to speak) its Christian equivalent. On the contrary, the real nature and significance of this new day was defined in relation to the sabbath and to the concept of time connected with it. The key position of the sabbath (and all its related prescriptions) in the Old Testament law and Hebrew piety is well known. From whatever source the weekly cycle of time may have been acquired by Israel, its religious interpretation and experience was rooted in a specifically biblical theology of time. The Seventh Day, the day of complete rest, is a commemoration of the creation of the world, a participation in the rest of God after creation. This rest signifies and expresses the fullness, the completion, the 'goodness' of the world, it is the eternal actualisation of the word spoken about the world by God from the beginning: 'It is very good.' The sabbath sanctions the whole natural life of the world unfolding through cycles of time, because it is the divinely instituted sign of the correspondence of the world to God's will and purpose. On this day the Law prescribes joy: 'Thou shalt eat and drink and give thanks to him who created all things,' since 'He who created all things honoured and sanctified the sabbath day and commanded that it should be so' (2 Macc 15:2-4). Faithfulness to the sabbath was bound up with the ultimate mystical depths of the people of Israel, and only by understanding it as something for which people were prepared to die, is it possible to comprehend the significance of the new day introduced by the church.

The Eighth Day is the day beyond the limits of the cycle outlined by the week and punctuated by the sabbath – this is the first day of the New Aeon, the figure of the time of the Messiah. 'And I have also established the eighth day,' we read in the book of Enoch, 'that the eighth day be the first after my creation, that in the beginning of the eighth millennium there be a time without reckoning, everlasting, without years, months, weeks, days or hours.'

From *Introduction to Liturgical Theology*, Faith Press, Leighton Buzzard, 1966.

Sixth Sunday of Lent

The Passion Narratives
Raymond E. Brown

Every year during Holy Week the liturgy of the church exposes us to a bit of biblical criticism by appointing two different passion narratives to be read within a short period. On Palm Sunday we hear the Passion according to Matthew, Mark or Luke, while on Good Friday every year we hear the Passion according to John. 'Those who have ears to hear' should notice that the two narratives which are read in a given year do not offer the same picture of the crucifixion of Jesus in either content or outlook.

When these different passion narratives are read side-by-side, one should not be upset by the contrast or ask which view of Jesus is more correct. All are given to us by the inspiring Spirit, and no one of them exhausts the meaning of Jesus. It is as if one walks around a large diamond to look at it from three different angles. A true picture of the whole emerges only because the viewpoints are different. In presenting two diverse views of the crucified Jesus every Holy Week, one on Palm Sunday, one on Good Friday, the church is bearing witness to that truth and making it possible for people with very different spiritual needs to find meaning in the cross. There are moments in the lives of most people when they need to cry out with St Matthew's Jesus, 'My God, My God, why have you forsaken me?' and to find, as Jesus did, that despite human appearances God is listening and can reverse tragedy. At other moments, meaning in suffering may be linked to being able to say with the Lucan

Jesus, 'Father, forgive them for they know not what they do,' and being able to entrust oneself confidently to God's hands. There are still other moments where with Johannine faith we must see that suffering and evil have no real power over God's Son or over those whom he enables to become God's children. To choose one portrayal of the crucified Jesus in a manner that would exclude the other portrayals or to harmonise all the gospel portrayals into one would deprive the cross of much of its meaning. It is important that some be able to see the head bowed in dejection, while others observe the arms outstretched in forgiveness, and still others perceive in the title on the cross the proclamation of a reigning king.

From *A Crucified Christ in Holy Week,* Collegeville, MN: The Liturgical Press, 1986. Used by kind permission of the publisher.

Monday of Holy Week

The Humility of God
John Macquarrie

The passion of Jesus Christ is not only a great human drama. Christians have seen in it the decisive moment when God himself has drawn near and made himself known. When we think of the passion and death of Jesus Christ, we are not primarily recalling the fate of an individual, however inspiring that may be. We are meditating on the mystery of God, for here, we believe, the ultimate reality is revealed at its deepest level. And what we learn about that reality is both shattering and strengthening.

It is shattering because it contradicts all our conventional ideas of God. It is no wonder that the cross is considered an offence. The lonely figure of Jesus Christ, following the way of the cross, seems not so much the revelation of God as rather the contradiction of everything that has been commonly believed about God. 'Almighty God' is our usual way of addressing him, and even Christians have tended to think of God as a celestial monarch, disposing of the world according to his sovereign will, untouched and untroubled by the storms that rage below. Some of our hymns of the passion encourage these ideas: 'The Father on his sapphire throne expects his own anointed Son.' This is surely a terrible misunderstanding. The point is that we are being invited to see God in the Son, in this despised, rejected, suffering figure, not to look away from him to some distant sapphire throne, as if the reality were there rather than here, and as if what we see on Calvary is a bad dream obscuring the reality. To think in that way would be to miss the whole meaning of incarnation and passion, which is that God comes among us in weakness and humility to stand with us in the midst of the created order.

Where we go wrong is that we bring along some ready-made idea of God, wherever we may have learned it, and then we try to make Jesus Christ fit in with that idea of God. If we take the idea of a revelation of God in Christ seriously, then we must be willing to have our understanding of God corrected and even revolutionised by what we learn in Jesus Christ. In other words, we cannot fit Christ into some previously established theistic understanding of the world. We have to move in the opposite direction, and this means that it is through Christ that we have to understand God and his relation to the world, so far as we can understand those matters. We have to begin with the cross, with what happened here on earth and in the course of human history, not with the exalted deity on the sapphire throne of pious imagining.

From *The Humility of God*, SCM Press Ltd, London, 1978. Used by kind permission of the publisher.

Tuesday of Holy Week

The Passion and the Spirit
John Macquarrie

When we consider the almost universal tendency to make power rather than love the defining characteristic of God, it is not surprising when we hear that in the ancient world Christians were ridiculed for worshipping a crucified God – the very idea seemed self-contradictory. Because of the difference of its God from other possible gods, the Christian faith has developed its own language for naming the mystery of God. The word 'God' by itself is too ambiguous and too prone to misunderstanding. Thus Christianity developed its own trinitarian language for speaking of God. God is Father, Son and Holy Spirit. Only some such conception comes anywhere near to being adequate to the God who is known in Christian faith. The triune God is no mere theological speculation, but is the church's attempt to spell out, in however faltering a way, something of the richness and distinctiveness of the specifically Christian experience of God.

So if we would understand the cross and passion of Christ on a deeper level, as revelation of God as well as human drama, we must try to think of these events in relation to the triune God. We shall then see how deeply the cross enters into the understanding of God, Father, Son and Holy Spirit, and that means into our understanding of the deepest reality there is.

In this threefold meditation on the passion in relation to the triune God, it is convenient to think of the persons of the Trinity in the reverse of the usual order, that is to say, we begin with God the Holy Spirit. We do so because the Holy Spirit is God in his nearness to us. The Spirit has proceeded or come forth from the Father into the creation. The Spirit is God, active and present in the whole created order and especially among human beings who are themselves spiritual and capable of responding to the Holy Spirit of God.

From the very beginning, the Holy Spirit has been in the creation and among humankind, sharing our suffering and striving for our liberation – and it is this picture of God the Spirit that gives us a juster understanding of God's nature than the picture of the sapphire throne. It is all of a piece with the cross and passion, for we can see the cross as the culmination in the Spirit-filled man, Jesus Christ, of that costly travail of the divine Spirit for the perfecting of the creation that has gone on through all the ages.

The Spirit is still sighing in our midst. Our meditation on the passion of Christ points to the passionate striving of the Spirit. 'Today if you will hear his voice, harden not your hearts.'

From *The Humility of God*, SCM Press Ltd, London, 1978. Used by kind permission of the publisher.

Wednesday of Holy Week

The Passion and the Son
John Macquarrie

Jesus Christ is 'the human face of God'. In him we meet God communicating himself to us in the medium of our own human existence.

To say that Christ is the human face of God is, of course, to assert nothing less than that he *is* God, and at an early stage in the history of the church Christians realised that one cannot worship Christ or attach ultimacy to his teachings or make for him the claims that Christians do make, if he is anything less than God. Theologically, Christ's relation to God found expression in the teaching which identified him with the second person of the Trinity. This second person of the Trinity, in turn, is understood as that mode of the divine being through which God creates an ordered world and relates himself to that world and so to the history and affairs of humankind.

Two metaphors have been traditionally used for the second person of the Trinity, and these both express the closeness, indeed, the identity of Christ with God. The first metaphor is sonship. We call Jesus Christ the Son of God, and a son is of the very flesh and blood of his father, a distinct being, yet at the same time an extension and continuation of the father's being. The second metaphor is language. We call Christ also the Word of God, and a word is not separable from the person who speaks it and whose mind it brings to expression. Thus to speak of Christ as Son of God or Word of God means that he is one in being or consubstantial with the Father.

There are two ways in which we can explore further the belief that the crucified Christ is the human face of God.

In the first approach, we begin from the consideration of what it means to be a human person. The human being is not a finished, ready-made product. Rather, we have to say that human beings are searching for their identity and trying to discover a true humanity. We are an open kind of being, open towards God. We bear obscurely within us the image of God. Christians believe that in Jesus Christ a true humanity did come to light and that in him the image of God was perfectly revealed.

But there is a second approach. It begins not from the deification of human beings but from the humanity of God, the humility of God. For God was putting something of himself into the creation from the beginning, and eventually must find perfect expression in the creation. The cross and passion are already there in God before the actual historical passion of Jesus of Nazareth. We could only think it incongruous that God should reveal himself in Jesus if we thought of God as other than a God of love. It is not incongruous if the creator is a God of love who in the act of creating committed himself to his creatures and resolved to stand beside them through all the risks and adventures of the creation's unfolding. God's servant-form was no mere disguise but a consequence of his love.

From *The Humility of God*, SCM Press Ltd, London, 1978. Used by kind permission of the publisher.

The Easter Triduum

Holy Thursday

The Eucharist
John D. Zizioulas

In his first letter to the Corinthians in connection with the
celebration of the Lord's Supper, Paul writes: 'The cup of
blessing which we bless is it not a communion (*koinonia*) of
the blood of Christ? The bread which we break is it not a
communion of the body of Christ? Because there is one
bread, we who are many are one body, for we all partake of
the one loaf.'

The idea of the incorporation of the 'many' into the
'one,' or of the 'one' as a representative of the 'many' goes
back to a time earlier than Paul. It is an idea basically connected with the figures of the 'Servant of God' and the 'Son
of Man.' But what is significant for us here is that this idea
was from the beginning connected with the eucharistic
consciousness of the church. Paul, in writing those words to
the Corinthians, was simply echoing a conviction apparently
widely spread in the primitive church.

Thus with regard to the tradition of the Servant of God
the texts of the Last Supper, in spite of their differences on
many points, agree on the connection of the Supper with
the 'many' for whom the 'one' offers himself. This relation
of the eucharist to the tradition of the Servant of God in
whom the many are represented established itself in the
liturgical life of the church already in the first century.

Coming together in brotherly love was certainly not a
Christian innovation. In the Roman Empire it was so
common to form 'associations' that there was need for

special laws concerning such. The brotherly love which prevailed was so strong and organised that each one would contribute monthly to a common fund and would address the other members by the title 'brethren'. Apart from the pagans, the Jews who lived in the Roman Empire were also organised in special communities under their own ethnarch, and their brotherly love was so strong that in cases of special groups, like the Essenes, it was based on principles of common property. To speak, therefore, of the unity of the early Christians in terms of brotherly love would be to miss the unique point of this unity. There was a basic difference in faith that distinguished Christians from their environment. Whereas the Jews based the unity of their gatherings on race, the pagans with their *collegia* or profession, the Christians declared that in Christ 'there is neither Jew nor Greek,' male or female, adult or child, rich or poor, master or slave.

This attitude which transcended not only social but also natural divisions (such as age, race, etc.) was portrayed in the eucharistic community *par excellence*.

From *Being as Communion* (Crestwood, NY: St Vladimir's Seminary Press, 1993; www.svspress.com). Used by kind permission of the publisher.

Good Friday

The Cross of Christ
Hugo Rahner

For the Jewish prophets, the tree of life in the centre of
Paradise, watered by the four rivers (Gen 2:9-10) was
already a symbol of Messianic salvation; indeed, this tree
was God's wisdom itself. In the same image, the author of
the New Testament Apocalypse saw the fulfillment of
redemption. But here a decisive new element is added: only
those who have washed their raiment in the blood of the
Lamb have 'right to the tree of life' (Rev 22:14). Between
the tree of life in paradise and the tree of life in the heaven
to come, the early Christian beheld a tree of life on which
the fate of the race of Adam was decided: the Cross. And
with their feeling for mystery, they saw these trees as a single
image. The tree of paradise is only a prefiguration of the
Cross, and the Cross is the centre of the world and of the
human drama of salvation. It rises from Golgotha to heaven,
embracing the cosmos; it is erected in the same place where
Adam was once created, where he lies buried, where at the
same day and hour the second Adam was to die. An early
Christian poem of the third century begins with the words:

> There is a spot that we believe the whole world's midpoint:
> The Jews in their mother tongue call it Golgotha.

Between these two trees, the early Christians saw the
tree of the Cross as the same tree of life on which our fate
as human beings was decided. In medieval art, Adam's skull
was represented at the foot of the cross, because they knew

that the cross was erected where Adam was created and was buried. Round it flowed the four rivers of paradise. On his deathbed, the legend went, Adam sent his son Seth to paradise to bring him the fruit of immortality from the tree of life. The angel gave him three seeds from which grew a threefold tree out of the dead Adam's mouth, made of cedar, pine and cypress. This is the tree that the soldiers cut down to make the cross of Christ. Such elaborate stories are part of the rich understanding and veneration of the Cross in early Christianity. Such mythological elaboration is a profound expression of the depth and the abundance of the understanding of this mystery as something so unique and so generous that it breaks through all attempt to classify it.

The third century Pseudo Chrysostom writes: 'Immortal tree, it extends from heaven to earth. It is the fixed pivot of the universe, the fulcrum of all things, the foundation of the world, the cardinal point of the cosmos. It binds together all the multiplicity of human nature. It is held together by invisible nails of the spirit in order to retain its bond with the Godhead. It touches the highest summits of heaven and with its feet holds fast the earth, and it encompasses the vast middle atmosphere in between with its immeasurable arms.'

From 'The Mystery of the Cross', *The Mysteries, Eranos Yearbooks 2,* Pantheon Books, Bollingen Series, 2, New York, 1955.

Holy Saturday

The Triumph of the Cross
Rainer Maria Rilke

I cannot conceive that the *cross* should *remain*, which was, after all, only a crossroads. It certainly should not be stamped on us on all occasions like a brand-mark. For is the situation not *this*: he intended simply to provide the loftier tree, on which we could ripen better. He, on the cross, is this new tree in God, and we were to be warm, happy fruit, at the top of it.

We should not always talk of what was *formerly*, but the *afterwards* should have begun. This tree, it seems to me, should have become so one with us, or we with it, and by it, that we should not need to occupy ourselves continually with it, but simply and quietly with God, for his aim was to lift us up into God more purely.

When I say: God, that is a great conviction in me, not something learnt. It seems to me, the whole creation speaks this word, without reflection, though often out of deep thoughtfulness. If this Christ has helped us to say it more fully, more effectually, with a clearer voice, so much the better, but now at last leave him out of the question. Do not always force us back into the labour and sorrow that it cost him to 'redeem' us. Let us, at last, enter into this state of redemption. Otherwise the situation of the Old Testament is certainly better, it is full of pointers towards God, wherever you open it. And God stands at the end towards which it points, in his eternal rising, in an East without end. Christ surely wanted the same thing. To point.

But the people here have been like dogs that do not understand the pointing finger and think that they are meant to
snap at the hand. Instead of setting out from the place of
the crossroads where this sign was high and lifted up into
the night of his sacrifice, instead of proceeding onwards
from this place of the cross, Christianity has settled down
there and claims that it is living there in Christ. But they
do not dwell in Christ, these stubborn of heart, who continually bring him back again and live from the setting up
of a cross. There was no room in him there, not even for his
mother, nor for Mary Magdalene, as there never is room in
anyone who points the way, who is a gesture and not a
dwelling-place. They have on their conscience this standing
around in an overcrowded place; it is their fault that the
journey does not begin to follow the direction of the arms
of the cross. They have made a *métier* out of Christian living,
a bourgeois occupation. Everything that they do of themselves, in harmony with their insuppressible nature (in so far
as they are still alive), is a contradiction of this strange situation,
and so they muddy their own waters and have to renew
them constantly. In their zeal, they do not hesitate to make
this life, which should be an object of desire and trust for
us, bad and worthless. What folly to direct our thoughts to a
Beyond, when we are surrounded here by tasks and expectations and future prospects! Does death really become less
opaque because these lighting devices have been dragged
into place behind it? Is this the reason why the cities are so
full of ugly artificial light and noise, because the true radiance
and song have been delivered over to a Jerusalem to be
inhabited later? The *right use* is the thing. To take a good

hold of this life, with warm affection and wonder, as our sole possession in the meantime; this is what Saint Francis of Assisi thought to write down in his song to the Sun, which was more glorious to him as he lay dying than was the cross, which only stood there to point into the sun. But the song of the dying man, drowned out on all sides, was heard only by a few simple monks, and infinitely confirmed by the landscape of his lovely valley.

From *Rodin and Other Prose Pieces*, Quartet Books, London, 1986. Used by kind permission of the publisher.

Easter Sunday

The Windhover
Gerard Manley Hopkins

To Christ our Lord

I CAUGHT this morning morning's minion, kingdom
of daylight's dauphin, dapple-dawn-drawn Falcon, in his
riding
Of the rolling level underneath him steady air, and
striding
High there, how he rung upon the rein of a wimpling
wing
In his ecstasy! then off, off forth on swing,
As a skate's heel sweeps smooth on a bow-bend: the
hurl and gliding
Rebuffed the big wind. My heart in hiding
Stirred for a bird – the achieve of; the mastery of the
thing!

Brute beauty and valour and act, oh, air, pride, plume, here
Buckle! AND the fire that breaks from thee then, a billion
Times told lovelier, more dangerous, O my chevalier!

No wonder of it: shéer plód makes plough down sillion
Shine, and blue-bleak embers, ah my dear,
Fall, gall themselves, and gash gold-vermillion.

The Season of Easter

Monday of Easter Week

The Event of the Resurrection
Hans Urs von Balthasar

Rightly enough, it has always been emphasised that there can have been no witnesses to the event of the Son's Resurrection by the Father – any more than there can to the act of the Incarnation. And yet the two actions are foundational events of a salvation which is for humanity, and God does not simply bring about these events without human beings, any more than he allowed the Passion to happen without human co-operation. Evidently, it is not enough for Mary to take cognisance after the event that she is pregnant, nor for the women to find the empty tomb after the act. Matthew felt that when – moving close to the border of mythology but not over-stepping that boundary – he made the women witnesses not, to be sure, of the Resurrection itself, but of the opening of the tomb by the angel of dazzling brightness.

Luke and John go, each in their own fashion, further still. That Resurrection and Ascension are substantially identical has been apparent in Luke. On the Mount of Olives, the disciples are witnesses of the disappearance from earth of him who is going to the Father – but only the disappearing remains within view, the cloud ensuring that the 'journey' enters the realm of the invisible. The Lucan disciples, therefore, 'see' the invisible end-point of the event whose point of departure Mary had 'seen' in her conversation with the angel of the Annunciation. They are testimonies to the final 'proof' (Acts 1, 3). In her own manner, Mary

Magdalen is also, on Easter morning, when she meets the Lord, in the event of the Resurrection. And Mary of Bethany, in her loving gesture of anticipation, accorded with all that the Lord decided, even with his burial, even with his Passion. For the three chief articulations of the redemption, the 'Yes' of the three Marys is required. Beyond all contestation they symbolise the believing and loving church. At the Ascension, the disciples 'were gazing into heaven,' seeking the One who had disappeared. And now the warning of the angel interpreter is reversed: 'Why do you stand looking into heaven?' Until the Lord's return, there is nothing more to see. The disciples are sent back to making their way throughout the world.

From *Mysterium Paschale*, T&T Clark, Edinburgh, 1990. Used by kind permission of Continuum International Publishing Group Ltd.

Tuesday of Easter Week

The Condition of the Risen One
Hans Urs von Balthasar

The condition of the Risen one is absolutely unique. This absolute uniqueness is theological in character, since in the greatest possible difference of conditions – deepest abasement and highest exaltation, God-abandonment and union with God – is expressed the supreme identity of the person. This identity, both of person and of his 'dispositions' (Philippians, 2:5), John expresses in the image of the slain Lamb upon the throne. In both phases, what is involved is the sovereignty and, indeed, the divinity of the Son's obedience as representation of the Trinitarian Love both in itself and for the world. But inasmuch as this unique event signifies the turning of the ages, and the foundation of the new world through the death of the old, one cannot decide how the Risen One will appear to his disciples. There is no point in setting up a determinate mode of appearance as norm for all the rest.

Through all the Resurrection stories runs the theme of the Lord's spontaneous self-revelation. What becomes manifest here is not only the freedom of the Risen One to offer himself when and as he wills, but also a leaving free of us to react just as we will. The Risen One has so mighty a freedom that, for the sake of the encounter, he communicates a part of this freedom to whomsoever he meets.

What the Spirit will manifest of the Son for history will always remain a sign of contradiction, and will never be imposed in a direct manner in the history of the world.

That God has manifested the Risen One, 'not to all the people, but to us who were chosen by God as witnesses' (Acts 10:41), and has given the faith of the nations the precarious foundation of this witness, is in itself not only daring, but also 'scandal and folly.' Jesus was able to make known the hidden God, who is faithful to his covenant till the end, only 'because he himself shared and shares the hiddenness of God.'

From *Mysterium Paschale*, T&T Clark, Edinburgh, 1990. Used by kind permission of Continuum International Publishing Group Ltd.

Wednesday of Easter Week

The Founding of the Church
Hans Urs von Balthasar

The interplay between the feminine and masculine representatives of the church at Easter, as that appears in the synoptic accounts, John deepens into an allegory which forms part of the ecclesiology of his two closing chapters. The Mother of Jesus is entrusted to the beloved disciple, and the author of the Apocalypse sees the church, as woman, give birth to the Messiah. He has a feeling for the femininity of the church in relation to the Lord. What is in question is the equilibrium between the church as 'bride' of Christ and the church as hierarchical institution. Paul allows the testimony of the women to fall out of the picture. He knows only appearances before males – first before Peter, and then, before the Twelve.

To this problem of the church as feminine and masculine is linked in John a developed allegory on the relation between the church as office in Peter and the church of love in John. Only the reader who sees the two apostles as real symbols of these two aspects of the church of Christ understands the evangelist's intention.

The two disciples run together towards the tomb. Love unencumbered as it is by burdens, 'runs ahead', whilst the hierarchical function, with its many preoccupations, reaches the goal later. Love sees what can be seen, yet allows authority to overtake it. Authority, looking at everything and seeing the napkin at the head rolled up in an orderly way, comes up with a kind of *nihil obstat* which lets love enter freely. This first episode suggests a church with two poles: the church of office and the church of love, with a harmonious tension between them, the official function working for love, love respectively allowing first place to office.

From *Mysterium Paschale*, T&T Clark, Edinburgh, 1990. Used by kind permission of Continuum International Publishing Group Ltd.

Thursday of Easter Week

Easter
Karl Rahner

The risen Lord has not moved out from earth's little hut.
For, as a matter of fact, he still has his body – in a definitive
and glorified state, yes, but still his body. It is a part of this
earth that belongs to the earth forever as a share of her
reality and her destiny. He has risen in order to reveal that
through his death the life of freedom and of bliss remains
forever rooted in earth's narrow confines and in her grief,
in the very centre of her heart.

What we call his resurrection – and unthinkingly take
to be his own private destiny – is only the first surface
indication that all reality, behind what we usually call
experience (which we consider so important), has already
changed in the really decisive depth of things. His resurrection
is like the first eruption of a volcano which shows that
God's fire already burns in the innermost depths of the
earth, and that everything shall be brought to a holy glow
in his light. He rose to show that this had already begun.
The new creation has already started, the new power of a
transfigured earth is already being formed from the world's
innermost heart, into which Christ descended by dying.
Futility, sin and death are already conquered in the innermost realm of all reality, and only the 'little while' (which
we call history 'AD') is needed until what has actually
already happened appears everywhere in glory, and not only
in the body of Jesus.

Because the waters of grief and guilt still flow on the

surface where we stand, we fancy that their source in the depths is not yet dried up. Because evil still carves new marks on the face of the earth, we conclude that in the deepest heart of reality love is dead. But these are only appearances, which we take for the reality of life. But he is there. He is the heart of this earthly world and the mysterious seal of its eternal validity.

That is why we children of the earth may love the earth; that is why we must love her, even when she terrifies us and makes us tremble with her misery and her destiny of death. For ever since Christ, through his death and resurrection, penetrated the earth for all time, her misery has become provisional and a mere test of our faith in her innermost mystery, which is the risen One himself.

From *The Eternal Year*, London, Burns & Oates, 1964. Used by kind permission of Continuum International Publishing Group Ltd.

Friday of Easter Week

The Rediscovery of Easter
Roger Greenacre

Easter has failed to touch the hearts and imaginations of Christian peoples in the West in the same way as Christmas. The popularity of Christmas is easily understandable: it can make some kind of appeal even to people whose Christian faith is minimal or non-existent, and it has collected to itself a wealth of folklore and tradition. But in the West it is also true that for Christians of every tradition the Passion has made more of an impact than the Resurrection. Certainly the Passion can make more of an impact on our human sensibilities, because suffering and death are basic and common human experiences, whereas resurrection from the dead is manifestly not.

The dangerous divorce of Cross and Resurrection is not only a matter affecting the liturgical and devotional life of the church; it has also had a baneful influence on the church's theology. Not so long ago theologians used to study the Redemption without mentioning the Resurrection at all. Christ's work of redemption was seen as consisting in his incarnation, his life and his death on the cross. When the Resurrection was mentioned, it was not to give it any part in our salvation but to show it as Christ's personal triumph over his enemies, and a kind of glorious counterblast to the years of humiliation he had endured to redeem us. In short, Christ's resurrection was shorn of the tremendous significance seen in it by the first Christian teachers, and relegated to the background of the redemptive scheme.

The 'rediscovery' of Easter has been the fruit of a number of convergent movements of renewal in the church. It has been due to the revival of biblical theology and the concern to understand the basic preaching of the apostolic church. It has been due also to the renewed study of the Greek and Latin Fathers. It has been due to the Liturgical Movement, in which connection it is right to single out one particular name, that of Odo Casel of the Benedictine Abbey of Maria-Laach, whose whole life was dedicated to the understanding of the theology of the Christian Mystery and its liturgical expression: he died with singular appropriateness in the night of Easter 1948 just after he had proclaimed as deacon the good news of the light of Christ – *Lumen Christi!*

Another influence has been the Ecumenical Movement. The Orthodox churches have not suffered from the divorce introduced between the Cross and the Resurrection in the West. It has been a revelation to Western Christians to attend their great Easter midnight services. To them as to the early Christians the conviction of Christ's Resurrection has been the sustaining and invigorating power in their life and witness. 'Christ is risen! He is risen indeed!' Perhaps it needs a radical revolution in our outlook and mentality before we can become thoroughly convinced of this, but such a revolution must be brought to pass.

From *The Sacrament of Easter*, Studies in Christian Worship 4, The Faith Press, London, 1965.

Saturday of Easter Week

Victory over Death
Olivier Clément

The victory over death is a victory over biological death, which is henceforward transformed into a 'passing over', part of a great momentum of resurrection which must culminate in the manifestation of the Kingdom. The cosmos will be transfigured, in a manner no longer secret and sacramental, but open and glorious. In this universal metamorphosis persons will assume a bodily splendour, like Christ's at his transfiguration on the mountain, or after his resurrection.

Therefore, and most important of all, victory over death is also victory over spiritual death, which we experience daily and in which, left to ourselves, we should risk being imprisoned forever. It is a victory over hell. It is the certainty that henceforward no one will be separated from God, but that all will be – indeed, in a mysterious fashion, already are – immersed in his love. Victory over hell – this is the wonderful message that the ancient church never ceased to proclaim: 'I have opened the gates that were bolted. I have shattered the bars of iron and the iron has become red-hot; it has melted at my presence; and nothing more has been shut, because I am the gate for all beings.'

And in the words of another 'Ode of Solomon':
Who can understand love
But he who loves?
I am united with my beloved,
My soul loves him.

Because I love the Son
I shall become a son.
To cling to him who dies no more
Is to become immortal.
He who delights in life
Shall be alive.

From *The Roots of Christian Mysticism*, New City Press, New York, 1993. Used by kind permission of the publisher.

Low Sunday

Faith without Sight
Demetrius Dumm

It is somewhat surprising to see Thomas featured so
prominently in the relatively brief Johannine account of the
post-resurrection appearances of Jesus. Thomas has cameo
roles earlier in the gospel where he is identified as the
'twin' and where he makes an abrupt and rather rash
suggestion that he and the other disciples should simply go
up to Jerusalem and die with Jesus. And it is he who asks
Jesus in what sense he is the way to salvation. He merits a
mention also in Chapter 21, where he is again identified as
the 'twin'.

Thomas may in fact have been a twin since his name
means 'twin' in Aramaic. It is more likely, however, that
Thomas was called a twin because he had a striking physical
resemblance to Jesus. In that case, his reluctance to believe
the report that Jesus had been seen alive would be John's
way of emphasising that no merely human advantage
counts for anything in one's relationship with the Lord. The
only thing that really matters is a living, dynamic faith
which is what finally enlightens Thomas and enables him to
cry out, 'My Lord and my God.' Only at this moment does
he really begin to 'look like' Jesus. Once again, John insists
on an ideal of personal and mystical union with Jesus.

Thomas was not there at the time when Jesus came to
the disciples on the evening of the first day of the week,
but he was told about it by the others; he had the possibility
of believing through hearing, but he rejected it, and said he

would only believe if he had tangible proof. We have been
prepared for this aspect of his character by the previous
occasions on which he has spoken: 'Lord, we do not know
where you are going; how can we know the way?' He
represents unbelief within the circle of the disciples. But
though Thomas is rebuked, the final statement of faith is
given to him; what he says goes beyond everything that has
been said earlier in the gospel and it brings us back to the
prologue. 'My Lord and my God' reminds us that John had
said at the beginning that 'the Word was God.' Failing to
believe and sticking out for proof go well with being chosen
to have the final word that best expresses the truth.

From *A Mystical Portrait of Jesus*, Collegeville, MN: The Liturgical
Press, 2001. Used by kind permission of the publisher.

Monday of the second week of Easter

The Book of Revelation
Elisabeth Schüssler Fiorenza

The Book of Revelation remains for many Christians a book with 'seven seals,' seldom read and often relegated to a curiosity in the Bible. For others it has become *the* book of the New Testament, full of predictions for the future and revelations about the present.

Biblical scholarship claims to have moved past such popular readings and to understand the eschatological teaching of the book in its historical context of Jewish apocalypticism. It is much divided, however, in the evaluation of this. As an apocalyptic work, Revelation is often considered as more Jewish than Christian in its form and theology because it preaches vengeance and judgement but not love.

Early Christian apocalyptic stands in continuity with Jewish apocalyptic but represents 'a new angle of refraction'. Redemption is understood in terms of Jewish theology as the exodus and liberation from slavery rather than as the redemption of individual souls.

The author of Revelation insists that the Lord of the world is not the emperor but Jesus Christ who has created an alternative reign and community to that of the Roman empire. Yet over and against a 'realised Christian eschatology,' Revelation maintains the early Christian apocalyptic on the 'not yet' of salvation.

The dramatic narrative of Revelation can best be envisioned as a conic spiral moving from the present to the eschatological future. It also could be likened to a dramatic

motion picture whose individual scenes portray the persons
or actions every time from a different angle while at the
same time adding some new light and colour to the whole.
In a similar fashion, John creates a 'literary vision' instead of
a sermon. Yet by creating such a literary composition John
seeks to motivate Christians in Asia Minor. The visions of
an alternative empire and world seek to encourage
Christians in the face of harassment and victimisation.

From *The Book of Revelation, Justice and Judgment*, Fortress
Press, Minneapolis, 1998. Used by kind permission of Augsburg
Fortress Publishers.

Tuesday of the second week of Easter

Revelation as Apocalypse
Richard Bauckham

John (and thereby his readers with him) is taken up into heaven in order to see the world from the heavenly perspective. He is given a glimpse behind the scenes of history so that he can see what is really going on in the events of his time and place. He is also transported in vision into the final future of the world, so that he can see the present from the perspective of what its final outcome must be, in God's ultimate purpose for human history. The effect of John's visions, one might say, is to expand his readers' world, both spatially (into heaven) and temporally (into the eschatological future), or, to put it another way, to open their world to divine transcendence. The bounds which Roman power and ideology set to the readers' world are broken open and that world is seen as open to the greater purpose of its transcendent Creator and Lord. It is not that the here-and-now are left behind in an escape into heaven or the eschatological future, but that the here-and-now look quite different when they are opened to transcendence.

The world seen from this transcendent perspective, in apocalyptic vision, is a kind of new symbolic world into which John's readers are taken as his artistry creates it for them. But really it is not another world. The righteous suffer, the wicked flourish: the world seems to be ruled by evil, not by God. Where is God's kingdom? The apocalyptists sought to maintain the faith of God's people in the one, all-powerful and righteous God , in the face of the harsh realities of evil in the world, especially the political evil of the oppression of God's faithful people by the great pagan empires. The answer to this problem was always, essentially, that, despite appearances, it is God who rules his creation and the time is coming soon when he will overthrow the evil empires and establish his kingdom. John's apocalypse in important ways shares that central apocalyptic concern.

From *The Theology of the Book of Revelation*, Cambridge University Press, 1993. Used by kind permission of the publisher.

Wednesday of the second week of Easter

Revelation as Christian Prophecy
Richard Bauckham

Virtually all we know about John, the author of
Revelation, is that he was a Jewish Christian prophet.
Evidently he was one of a circle of prophets in the churches
of the province of Asia, and he had at least one rival: the
Thyatiran prophetess whom he considers a false prophet.
Thus to understand this book we must situate it in the
context of early Christian prophecy. John must normally
have been active as a prophet in the churches to which he
writes. The seven messages to the churches reveal detailed
knowledge of each local situation and the reading we have
just heard presumably refers to an earlier prophetic oracle
of his, addressed to the prophetess he calls Jezebel at
Thyatira.

Since Christian prophets normally prophesied in the
context of Christian worship meetings, we must assume
that this was what John usually did. The reading of this
written prophecy in the worship service was therefore a
substitute for John's more usual presence and prophesying
in person. Usually in the early churches prophets delivered
oracles which were given to them by God in the worship
meeting. They declared the revelation as they received it. It
took the form of a word of God spoken to the church,
under the inspiration of the Spirit, in the name of God or
the risen Christ, so that the 'I' of the oracle was the divine
person addressing the church through the prophet. But
early Christian prophets seem also to have received visionary

revelations which they conveyed to the church later in the form of a report of the vision. The vision was initially a private experience, even if it happened during the worship service, and was only subsequently reported to the church as prophecy. The whole book of revelation is a report of visionary revelation, but it also includes oracular prophecy within it. This occurs in the prologue, the epilogue, and the seven messages to the churches, which are oracles written as Christ's word to these churches.

From *The Theology of the Book of Revelation*, Cambridge University Press, 1993. Used by kind permission of the publisher.

Thursday of the second week of Easter

Authenticity of the Apocalypse
Raymond E. Brown

The issue of Revelation's relationship to the Johannine tradition is complicated. Certainly it should not be considered a Johannine writing in the sense in which that designation is applied to the gospel and epistles of John. Yet there are interesting parallels to elements in the Johannine literature, especially the gospel, that suggest a relationship. Nevertheless, such similarities are far less than those between the gospel and the epistles of John. Consequently, in the view of the majority of scholars one does not have justification for speaking of the author of Revelation as a member of the Johannine school of writers who wrote the body of the gospel, the epistles, and redacted the gospel. To do justice to all the factors, however, one should probably posit some contact between the seer and the Johannine tradition or writings.

In antiquity there were problems about the canonicity of Revelation, in part in relation to whether or not John (the apostle) was thought to be the author. The book was widely accepted in the Western churches. In Asia Minor toward the end of the 2nd century, opposition to Montanist beliefs about a new outpouring of the Spirit caused the Alogoi to reject Revelation as well as John. Elsewhere in the East, once Dionysius of Alexandria, in around 250 CE, showed that Revelation was not written by John the apostle, the work was often rejected. Nevertheless, Revelation was accepted in the 4th century by Athanasius, and eventually the Greek-speaking church came to accept it. However, it continued to be rejected in Syria and by the Syriac-speaking church. In Reformation times, Luther assigned Revelation to a secondary status; Zwingli denied that it was scripture; and it was the only New Testament book on which Calvin did not write a commentary. Today there is no major problem of a denial of canonical status. However, Revelation is overused in the wrong way, and reaction to such overuse sometimes prevents others from seeing its genuine value. It may well be important, then, to propose for discussion a strong clarifying statement – one that will scandalise some Christians, but is acceptable to the majority, and which implies no rejection of inspiration or revelation. God has not revealed to human beings details about how the world began or how the world will end, and failing to recognise that, one is likely to misread both the first book and the last book in the Bible. The author of Revelation did not know how or when the world will end, and neither does anyone else.

From *An Introduction to the New Testament*, Yale University Press, 1997. Used by kind permission of the publisher..

Friday of the second week of Easter

Jewish & Christian Apocalyptic
Raymond E. Brown

Our oldest illustration of biblical apocalyptic, and one indicative of its beginnings, may be dated to the Babylonian exile. That catastrophe, following the capture of Jerusalem, destruction of the Temple, and fall of the monarchy, began to call into question the possibility of salvation within history. Although the Book of Ezekiel is dominantly prophetic in the sense that the prophet expected deliverance in history, the extravagant imagery of his visions and his idealistic anticipation of the New Israel virtually go beyond history and overlap into apocalyptic style and anticipation. Indeed, Ezekiel supplied a major part of apocalyptic language and images that would be used in the future: the four living creatures, lion, ox and eagle, with one looking like a man; an enthroned figure above the firmament described in terms of gems and precious metals, eating scrolls, the harlot, the wicked prosperous city-kingdom blasphemous in its arrogance, Gog of Magog, measuring the Temple etc. A combination of prophetic historical message with apocalyptic elements and imagery is found in the Book of Joel, of uncertain date but probably postexilic. From the same general period comes Zechariah with his visions (interpreted by an angel) of lampstands, scrolls, four different coloured horses; and from sometime later come deutero Zechariah and trito Zechariah, with an allegory of the shepherds and pictures of judgement and an Ideal Jerusalem.

Another important period for the appearance of apocalyptic writing was the 3rd and 2nd centuries BC when the Greek dynasties of the Ptolemies in Egypt and the Seleucids in Syria, descended from Alexander the Great's conquest, became more authoritarian in their rule of Judea. In particular the persecution of the Jewish religion in favour of the worship of the Greek gods under the Seleucid king, Antiochus IV Epiphanes sharpened a sense of diabolic evil that only God could overcome. The idea of an afterlife had now developed clearly among some Jews, and that opened the possibility of eternal happiness replacing an existence marked by suffering and torture. In this period we move from prophetic books with apocalyptic traits to full-fledged apocalypses. The initial section of I Enoch was composed in the 3rd century BC, and to the treasury of apocalyptic symbolism it contributed pictures of the final judgement and of wicked angels who fall and are locked up till the last days. A later section of the book lays out pre-determined history in a pattern of weeks. Dan, the greatest Old Testament biblical apocalypse, was written around 165 BC. The vision of four monstrous beasts followed by the heavenly coronation of a son of man and the vision of the seventy weeks of years had a strong impact on later apocalypses. We do not know whether the author of Revelation knew Jesus' long apocalyptic discourse in Mark 13 for instance, but he knew traditional apocalyptic elements that circulated among 1st century Christians.

From *An Introduction to the New Testament*, Yale University Press, 1997. Used by kind permission of the publisher.

Saturday of the second week of Easter

The Eighth Day
Alexander Schmemann

Christ rose not on the sabbath, but on the first day of the week. The sabbath was the day of his rest, his 'en-sabbath-ment' in the tomb, the day which completed his task within the limits of the 'old aeon'. But the new life, the life which had begun to 'shine out of the tomb,' began on the first day of the week. This was the first day, the beginning of the risen life over which 'death has no dominion'. This day also became the day of the Eucharist as the 'confession of his res-urrection,' the day of the communication to the church of this risen life. In early Christianity, this day was often called 'the eighth day'. St Basil writes: 'The Lord's Day is great and glorious. The scripture knows this day without evening, having no other day, a day without end; the psalmist calls it the eighth day, since it is outside of time measured in weeks.' In this way the eighth day is defined in opposition to the week. The week is related to time. The eighth day is outside time. The week stands within the sequence of days, the eighth day has nothing coming after it, it is the 'last one'.

In the church the first-eighth day, the Lord's Day, is the day of the Eucharist. The early Christian tradition bears uniform witness to this fact. The Eucharist has its day, Christians gather together on an established day. We know that the 'Day of the Sun' was not a holy day of rest in either the Jewish or the Roman calendars. The Eucharist is the sacrament of the church. It is the parousia, the presence of the Risen and Glorified Lord in the midst of 'his own,' those who in him constitute the church and are already 'not of this world' but partakers of the new life of the New Aeon. The day of the Eucharist is the day of the 'actualisation' or manifestation in time of the day of the Lord as the kingdom of Christ. The early church did not connect either the idea of repose or the idea of a natural cycle of work and rest with the Eucharistic Day of the Lord. Constantine established this connection with his sanction of the Christian Sunday. For the church the Lord's Day is the joyful day of the kingdom. The Lord's Day signifies for her not the substitution of one form of reckoning time by another, the replacement of Saturday by Sunday, but a break into the 'New Aeon,' a participation in a time that is by nature totally different.

The eschatology of the new Christian cult does not mean the renunciation of time. There would have been no need for a fixed day (*statu die*) in a 'wholly world-renouncing' cult; it could be celebrated on any day and at any hour. Nor does this eschatology become related to time through the sanctification of one of the days of the week, like the sabbath in the Old Testament law. The 'Lord's Day' actualised in the Eucharist was not 'one of the ordinary sequence of days'. Just as the church herself while existing in 'this world' manifests a life which is 'not of this world,' so also the 'Lord's Day,' while it is actualised within time on a given day, manifests within this sequence that which is above time and belongs to another aeon.

From *Introduction to Liturgical Theology*, Faith Press, Leighton Buzzard, 1966.

Third Sunday of Easter

The Way to Emmaus
Nicholas Lash

The theological task of every age is not simply the proclamation, but, as Eamon Duffy has said, the *recognition* of the truth it has received. Christian truth is not 'religious' truth, but truth sacramentally displayed and exhibited. And it is *all* facts and circumstances which require interpretation in the light of the mystery of Christ crucified and risen.

The story of the disciples on the way to Emmaus can serve as a parable for the task of Christian interpretation. Those disciples, like the rest of us, had some difficulty in 'reading' their history, and the context of 'recognition', the occasion on which things began to make sense, was not some 'religious' event in a sacred space, but an act of human hospitality.

That context is today, as it has always been, a community of disciples on a journey, their memory shaped by a particular darkness, who talk with each other about these things that happen; a community who, then as now, are accompanied, and who, although they often cannot understand their company, are still enabled to recognise him in the breaking of bread.

If Christianity could unlearn its own incoherent juxtaposition of historical pessimism and eschatological optimism, and could instead recover and sustain the precariousness of its hope, it might proclaim the message of the resurrection of the flesh more effectively.

The focal point of both memory and hope is Gethsemane and Calvary. It was there that God died, and resurrection began. To understand all places of darkness and death to be that garden and that hilltop is, therefore, to refuse to give the last word to all that entombs the body and the mind. Jesus taught us to address the darkness as 'Father'. But we only learn appropriately to do so at the place where he did it. It is only there, at the heart of darkness, that we are enabled and entitled to pray: 'All shall be well and all shall be well and all manner of thing shall be well.'

From *Theology on the Way to Emmaus*, SCM Press, London, 1986. pp xi-xii; 201; 214-215. Used by kind permission of the author.

Monday of the third week of Easter

The Seal of Everlasting Love
Karl Rahner

It is common knowledge how difficult and mysterious the Revelation of St John seems to be. But much of the obscurity is only apparent. If we realise the kind of language that is used here, we can much more easily distinguish between the imagery and what the image means. The seer is looking into his own time and into his Christian life; and enlightened by the Spirit of God and his own Christian experience, he looks into the future and sees as far as the end. He sees his present and the future of Christianity in a single perspective. He is not a reporter, relating one event after another in chronological order; we cannot apply the particular things he says to any definite historical events in the future. Rather, he keeps seeing one and the same thing in massive imagery – the crucial struggle that goes on throughout the history of the world and ends in eternal victory for God. This one thing is said over and over again. He sees that God is holding a book in his hand, a book sealed with seven seals. It is the book of universal history, the book of creation and time. Nobody can break the seals of this book or scroll, except the Lamb that was slain, the Crucified, the Son of God, who is the meaning of history, who came into history and experienced and suffered all that has ever happened, as the crucified and risen Lord.

Before we look into the book of universal history with its seven seals, we should be told that God has sealed those he calls into history, with the mark of his love. Then that history can be endured. It is obscure, and one might almost say that God should rather give us an account of our life than call us to account for it; for he isGod and must therefore answer for our existence. But he has told us – and what other answer could there be for us in time, in this imperfect life, upon our shadowed journey – he has told us that he has sealed us with the seal of his eternal love and that he sends down no road that will not lead to him, puts us into no history that will not end in his beatitude, calls no one into existence who is not chosen and sealed with God's eternal love.

From *Biblical Homilies*, Herder & Herder, London, 1966.

Tuesday of the third week of Easter

The Book of Revelation
J. B. Phillips

The most obvious and striking feature of the book of
Revelation at first sight is the oddness of the Greek in
which it is written. The difference in style between, let us
say, Luke's gospel and Paul's epistle to the Romans is very
marked. But when one is confronted with the language of
Revelation it is no mere difference of style which makes
one gasp, but crudities, grammatical errors and a quite
extraordinary juxtaposition of words. So wholly different is
the book in its word-usage and composition from the
Fourth Gospel that many scholars find themselves unable to
believe that both could be written by the same person. The
Fourth Gospel is written, within its limited vocabulary,
smoothly and correctly and would probably have caused no
literary qualms in a contemporary Greek reader. But
Revelation piles word upon word remorselessly, mixes cases
and tenses without apparent scruple, and shows at times a
complete disregard for normal syntax and grammar. The last
verse from the passage we have just heard read (8:13), translated literally, would have sounded as follows to an educated
reader of the first century:

> And I saw, and I heard one eagle flying in
> mid-heaven saying in a loud voice,
> 'Alas, alas, alas for the inhabitants upon
> the earth from the remaining voices of the
> trumpet of the three angels about to sound the trumpet!'

And such an example could be multiplied again and again. But the tumultuous assault of words is not without its effect upon the mind. The inspired words pour forth in a stream both uninhibited and uncorrected. The writer's mind was plainly steeped in the spirit and in the knowledge of Jewish apocalyptic. There is hardly a single direct quotation from the Old Testament but there are scores of parallels, echoes and recollections of it. John's words give the strong impression of one whose thoughts and thought-forms are Hebrew. My suggestion is that the writer, who had a genuine ecstatic experience, wrote down what he saw during the visions. If we suppose this to be true and if we suppose also that the writer were wholly convinced that what he had written was in fact written while 'in the spirit', then we can reasonably imagine that he would shrink from correction or revision lest he distort or modify the revelation he had been given.

From *The Book of Revelation*, Fontana Books, London, 1960. Used by kind permission of the publisher.

Wednesday of the third week of Easter

The Poetry of the Book of Revelation
J. B. Phillips

The crowns, the thrones, the gold, the jewels, the colours, the trumpets, the violence of action and the impact of incredible numbers and awe-inspiring size – all these images stir that threshold of the brain where monsters lurk and supernatural glories blaze. John is stirring with a kind of surrealistic artistry the vastnesses of our unconscious minds. The figures created in the mind are vivid and powerful enough to transport us to another spiritual dimension. Once we are gripped by the mysterious compulsion of these visions we find the 'silence in heaven for what seemed to be about half-an-hour' almost intolerable. The 'solitary eagle flying in mid-air,' crying out in pity for the inhabitants of the earth is, out of its context, bizarre to the point of absurdity, but, set as it is, it is almost unbearably poignant. And how beautifully right, how poetically satisfying it is to read that the leaves of the Tree of Life in the New Jerusalem are for the healing of the nations! The poetic impact of the book carries us away to a realm where the pedestrian rules of grammar no longer apply – we are dealing with celestial poetry and not with earthly prose. To be literal-minded and studiously analytical in such a work is to kill poetic truth. Dissection is not infrequently the death of beauty.

Almost any poem can be made to look ridiculous by having its superficial meaning reduced to ordinary prose. This by no means proves that a poem is bad poetry; on the contrary it emphasises the proper use of poetry which, by indefinable subtleties of rhythm, rhyme, and cadence, can strike chords and overtones forever beyond the reach of the finest prose.

From *The Book of Revelation*, Fontana Books, London, 1960. Used by kind permission of the publisher.

Thursday of the third week of Easter

Understanding the Imagery
Richard Bauckham

Consider the descriptions of the plagues of the seven trumpets and the seven bowls. These form a highly schematised literary pattern which itself conveys meaning. Their content suggests, among many other things, the plagues of Egypt which accompanied the exodus, the fall of Jericho to the army of Joshua, the army of locusts depicted in the prophecy of Joel, the Sinai theophany, the contemporary fear of invasion by Parthian cavalry, the earthquakes to which the cities of Asia Minor were rather frequently subject, and very possibly the eruption of Vesuvius which had recently terrified the Mediterranean world. John has taken some of his contemporaries' worst experiences and worst fears of wars and natural disasters, blown them up to apocalyptic proportions, and cast them in biblically allusive terms. The point is not to predict a sequence of events. The point is to evoke and to explore the meaning of the divine judgement which is impending on the sinful world.

The imagery of Revelation requires close and appropriate study if modern readers are to grasp much of its theological meaning. Misunderstandings of the nature of the imagery and the way it conveys meaning account for many misinterpretations of Revelation. Because Revelation does not contain theological discourse or argument of the kind with which readers of the New Testament are familiar, it should not be thought to be any less a product of profound theological reflection. Its images are by no means a vaguer or more impressionistic means of expression than the relatively more abstract conceptual argument of a pauline letter. They are capable both of considerable precision of meaning and of compressing a wealth of meaning into a brief space by evoking a range of associations. The method and conceptuality of the theology of Revelation are relatively different from the rest of the New Testament, but once they are appreciated in their own right, Revelation can be seen to be not only one of the finest literary works of the New Testament, but one of the greatest theological achievements of early Christianity.

From *The Theology of the Book of Revelation*, Cambridge University Press, 1993. Used by kind permission of the publisher.

Friday of the third week of Easter

Clashing of Symbols
Richard Bauckham

The unusual profusion of visual imagery in Revelation
provides its capacity to create a symbolic world which its
readers can enter and thereby have their perception of the
world in which they live transformed. To appreciate the
importance of this we should remember that Revelation's
readers in the great cities of the province of Asia were
constantly confronted with powerful images of the Roman
vision of the world. Civic and religious architecture,
iconography, statues, rituals and festivals, even the visual
wonder of cleverly engineered 'miracles' in the temples, as
described in the text we have just heard, all provided
powerful visual impressions of Roman imperial power and
the splendour of pagan religion. In this context, Revelation
provides a set of Christian prophetic counter-images which
impress on its readers a different vision of the world: how it
looks from the heaven to which John is caught up. The
visual power of the book effects a kind of purging of the
Christian imagination, refurbishing it with alternative
visions of how the world is and will be.

The images of Revelation are symbols with evocative
power inviting imaginative participation in the book's
symbolic world. But they do not work merely by painting
verbal pictures. Their precise literary composition is always
essential to their meaning. The composition of the book
creates a complex network of literary cross-references,
parallels, contrasts, which inform the meaning of the parts

and the whole. Not all of these will be noticed on the first or seventh or seventieth reading. They are one of the ways in which the book is designed to yield its rich store of meaning progressively through intensive study. Secondly, Revelation is saturated with verbal allusions to the Old Testament. These are not incidental but essential to the way meaning is conveyed. Without noticing some of the key allusions, little if anything of the meaning of the images will be understood. But like the literary patterning, John's very precise and subtle use of Old Testament allusions creates a reservoir of meaning which can be progressively tapped.

From *The Theology of the Book of Revelation*, Cambridge University Press, 1993. Used by kind permission of the publisher.

Saturday of the third week of Easter

How to read the Apocalypse
Raymond E. Brown

Revelation is widely popular for the wrong reasons, for a great number of people read it as a guide to how the world will end, assuming that the author was given by Christ detailed knowledge of the future that he communicated in coded symbols. For example, preachers have identified the Beast from the Earth whose number is 666 as Hitler, Stalin, the Pope, and Saddam Hussein, and have related events in Revelation to the Communist Revolution, the atom bomb, the creation of the State of Israel, the Gulf War, etc. The 19th and 20th centuries saw many interpreters of prophecy who used calculations from Revelation to predict the exact date of the end of the world. Up to the moment all have been wrong! Some of the more militant exponents have aggravated law-enforcement authorities to the point of armed intervention, as in the case of the Branch Davidians in Waco, Texas. On the other hand, many believing Christians do not think that the author knew the future in any sense beyond the absolute conviction that God would triumph by saving those who remained loyal and by defeating the forces of evil.

How can Revelation be presented in a way that is both factual and meaningful?

To a contemporary culture that idolises science and calculable knowledge, apocalyptic is an enduring witness to a reality that defies all our measurements; it testifies to another world that escapes all scientific gauges and finds expression in symbols and visions. That world is not created by imagination, but images serve as an entrée. Artists ranging from Brueghel through William Blake to Salvador Dalí have understood that. On a psychological level Jung sought an entry into that world through symbols. On a religious level mystics have offered insight. Liturgy, properly understood, brings ordinary believers into contact with this heavenly reality. To a world that accepts only what it can see, hear, and feel, Revelation is the final scriptural gateway to what the eye has not seen and the ear not heard. Because its visions are filled with theological symbols, not with photographic reproductions, Revelation does not give an exact knowledge of that other world, a world that cannot be translated into human concepts. Rather, it attests forcefully that at every moment of human history, even the most desperate moment that causes people to lose hope, God is present.

From *An Introduction to the New Testament*, Yale University Press, 1997. Used by kind permission of the publisher.

Fourth Sunday of Easter

The Good Shepherd
John Henry Newman

In those countries of the East where our Lord appeared, the office of a shepherd is not only a lowly and simple office, and an office of trust, as it is with us, but, moreover, an office of great hardship and of peril. Our flocks are exposed to no enemies, such as our Lord describes. The hireling shepherd is not tried. But where our Lord dwelt in the days of his flesh it was otherwise. There it was true that the good Shepherd giveth his life for the sheep.

Hence it was prophesied under this figure by the Prophet Isaiah, 'He shall feed his flock like a shepherd: he shall gather the lambs with his arm, and carry them in his bosom, and shall gently lead those that are with young' (Isa 11:10, 11). And, again, he promises by the mouth of Ezekiel, 'Behold, I, even I, will both search my sheep, and seek them out. As a shepherd seeketh out his flock in the day that he is among his sheep that are scattered; so will I seek out my sheep, and will deliver them out of all places where they have been scattered in the cloudy and dark day' (Ezek 34:11, 12). And the Psalmist says of him, 'The Lord is my Shepherd, therefore can I lack nothing. He shall feed me in a green pasture, and lead me forth beside the waters of comfort' (Ps 23:1, 2).

And hence, in like manner, from the time of Adam to that of Christ, a shepherd's work has been marked out with special Divine favour, as being a shadow of the good Shepherd who was to come. 'Righteous Abel' was 'a keeper of sheep'. And who were they to whom the Angels first brought the news that a Saviour was born? 'Shepherds abiding in the field, keeping watch over their flock by night.' (Luke 2:8).

But there are three favoured servants of God in particular, special types of the Saviour to come, men raised from low estate to great honour, in whom it was his will that his pastoral office should be thus literally fulfilled. And the first is Jacob, the father of the patriarchs, who appeared before Pharaoh. The second is Moses, who drove away the rival shepherds and helped the daughters of the Priest of Midian to water their flock; and who, while he was keeping the flock of Jethro, his father-in-law, saw the Angel of the Lord in a flame of fire in a bush. And the third is David, the man after God's own heart. He was 'the man who was raised on high, the anointed of the God of Jacob, and the sweet Psalmist of Israel' (2 Sam 23:1). but he was found among the sheep.

My brethren, we say daily, 'We are his people, and the sheep of his pasture.' Again, we say, 'We have erred and strayed from thy ways, like lost sheep.' Let us never forget these truths; let us never forget, on the one hand, that we are sinners; let us never forget, on the other hand, that Christ is our Guide and Guardian. He is our Shepherd, and the sheep know his voice. If we are his sheep, we shall hear it, recognise it, and obey it.

From *Parochial and Plain Sermons*, Vol 8, sermon 16.

Monday of the fourth week of Easter

The Beast from the Earth
Eugenio Corsini

Both beasts are the effect of the wicked action of Satan in two different human areas: political and religious, which John symbolically describes as 'sea' and 'earth'. In this sense their origins are contemporaneous and independent of one another, even if their development as presented is closely tied together, interdependent and complementary.

The explanation of the beast from the earth has not created great difficulties for the commentators, even though they have undervalued its importance. Most see it as a sort of 'spiritual double' of the first beast. Most see the first beast as Rome, they see the second as pagan cult, or more specifically the cult of Emperor worship, the mystery religions or magic practices. These interpretations are not entirely wrong, but they are too limited and precise. It is clear that this beast has an activity in the area of the psychological and spiritual, in an attempt to lead people to accept the domination of the first beast which represents political authority. While the activity of the beast from the sea is described by John through images of brute force and violence, the beast from the land acts more subtly, through the temptation to error which arises in the human mind and from natural attachment to human comfort. In the beast from the land we can see hints of what we would call the techniques of propaganda. There is no doubt that John could have seen the superb example of the religious, cultural and administrative organisation of the Roman Empire of his time. But this does not appear for the first time with the Roman Empire. The whole of the Bible is full of condemnations of kings who wished to take upon themselves divine authority, and impose themselves upon their subjects as such. The book of Daniel, a great favourite of our author, portrays two of them: Nebuchadnezzar and Antiochus IV. These are placed at the beginning and at the end of the great crises which will precede the coming of the Messiah, at the beginning and at the end of the famous seventy weeks.

Thus John is not concerned with the Roman Empire. In fact, the sign of the cult rendered to earthly sovereigns is the erection of a statue, and John uses this example often, and it clearly refers to the historical actions of Nebuchadnezzar and Antiochus IV. The former put up an immense golden statue and demanded that his subjects adore it, while the second had a statue to Zeus placed in the Temple, thus profaning it. Even if John saw the cult offered to the Roman Emperor, this would only confirm his conviction, which he had from the Word of God, that the desire to be adored was a constant fact in political authority which had been corrupted.

The identification of the second beast with the cult and priesthood of the pagans is therefore not quite as clear as many would think. What was in the Romans, had already been present in the Canaanites, the Egyptians, the Phoenicians, the Babylonians, and all of this had been condemned in the Old Testament. So the demands for adoration of a human political authority, and the persecution which met refusal, cannot be simply limited to the Roman Empire.

From *The Apocalypse*, Good News Studies, 5, Veritas, Dublin 1983. Used by kind permission of the publisher.

Tuesday of the fourth week of Easter

The Old Story & the New Story
Adela Yarbro Collins

The 'old story' evoked by the traditional images in the Apocalypse is the ancient story of cosmic combat. There were many stories of combat in the ancient Mediterranean world, but they shared certain basic features. The story usually begins with the rebellion of a divine or cosmic beast against the young creator god who maintains order in nature and among people. Sometimes the beast, often a dragon, wins at first, but ultimately the hero-god is victorious and reestablishes order in the world. The power and meaning of these stories cannot be reduced to a single interpretation or even expressed very well in abstract concepts. They grasp the imagination, evoke a response and have many connotations. St George battling the dragon is a story of this type which has remained in living memory up to the present. One important function of these stories is to express in a vivid and concrete way the perennial struggle between life and death, fertility and sterility, order and chaos. The dragon, for example, is a powerful symbol of the chaotic force which threatens to disrupt nature and destroy humanity.

The 'new story' of the Apocalypse is concerned with the confrontation between the followers of Jesus and the Roman empire. The expected hostility on the part of Rome is interpreted as the rebellion of chaos against the divine order. The polarity in the natural world expressed by the combat story is associated in the 'new story' of the Apocalypse primariliy with human society and the supernatural realm. The new polarity borders on dualism. All humanity is divided into followers of Christ and worshippers of the Roman empire. The Roman emperor is described as an Antichrist. It is implied that Satan rebels against God. This polarity expressed and reinforced the fundamental alienation of the prophet John and probably his first readers from the political order determined by Rome and even from the world as they experienced it. The worshippers of Rome are equated with the dwellers on earth. A basic solidarity of the earth with the social realm is presumed. Thus the earth must be destroyed before the new age can dawn.

From *The Apocalypse*, Veritas, Dublin, 1979. Used by kind permission of the publisher.

Wednesday of the fourth week of Easter

The Song of Moses
Richard Bauckham

In this passage the new exodus motif is used to depict the effect of the church's witness to the nations. The martyrs are seen to have come triumphantly out of their conflict with the beast. Their passage through martyrdom to heaven is compared with the passage of the Israelites through the Red Sea, for the sea of glass in heaven is now mingled with the fire of divine judgement. They stand beside the sea, praising God for the victory he has wrought for them, just as the people of Israel, led by Moses, sang a song of praise to God for his deliverance of them from Pharaoh's army. Because the new exodus is the victory the martyrs have won by the blood of the Lamb, their song is not only the song of Moses but also the song of the Lamb.

The significance of this version of the song of Moses is considerable. It shifts the emphasis of the new exodus from an event by which God delivers his people by judging their enemies to an event which brings the nations to acknowledge the true God. The martyrs celebrate the victory God has won through their death and vindication, not by praising him for their own deliverance, but by celebrating its effect on the nations, in bringing them to worship God. This gives a fresh significance to the use of new exodus imagery with reference to the first stage of Christ's work, in which by his death he ransomed a people from all the nations to be God's own people. We now see that this redemption of a special people from all the peoples is not an end in itself, but has a further purpose: to bring all the peoples to acknowledge and worship God. In the first stage of his work, the Lamb's bloody sacrifice redeemed a people for God. In the second stage, this people's participation in his sacrifice, through martyrdom, wins all the peoples for God. This is how God's universal kingdom comes.

From *The Theology of the Book of Revelation*, Cambridge University Press, 1993. Used by kind permission of the publisher.

Thursday of the fourth week of Easter

The Mystery of the Temple
Yves Congar

The whole meaning of the temple as it is understood by the gospel and the apostles is restated in the Apocalypse. The gospel meaning is that Christ (immolated and risen from the dead) is the temple. The meaning in the teaching of the apostles is that the temple is the community of the faithful. The Apocalypse, in its own key and with its own resonances, repeats the same theme. Christ is the Lamb slain and victorious, from whose side flows, as from the new Temple, the water of life, that is, the Spirit.

The community of the faithful, represented as militant on earth and in heaven as the liturgical assembly of those whose pilgrimage has ended in joy, is now God's dwelling-place. John sees the bridal city coming down from heaven, sees the new Jerusalem, and the voice of an angel which explains what is happening: 'Here is God's tabernacle pitched among us; he will dwell with us …' Yet, as in 1 Peter and Ephesians, the church is the temple only through Jesus Christ.

The Apocalypse includes and fulfills the cosmic aspect of the mystery of the temple. Christ is the source of a new creation, whose origin is the kingship of God which is shared by the Lamb who sits upon the same throne. At the root of all this is the theology of the prologue to St John's gospel whose keyword appears in Revelation 19:13. The longing for cosmic redemption is only fulfilled in the concrete economy of the incarnate Word, the Cross and Easter.

Hence the celestial city is given twelve gates, not by deduction from geophysics as in the case of modern Cambodian or Burmese symbolism, or in that of Moslem Baghdad with its twelve palaces. No, it is because there were twelve sons of Jacob, twelve tribes of Israel; and also twelve foundations since there were twelve apostles of the Lamb. A genuine cosmic value is implied, incorporated into the positive facts of the history of salvation, itself dependent upon a free act of God's will, by which moreover the world has been created as an ordered and measured whole.

From *The Mystery of the Temple*, Burns and Oates, London, 1962. Used by kind permission of Continuum International Publishing Group Ltd.

Friday of the fourth week of Easter

The Great Harlot
Richard Bauckham and Adela Yarbro Collins

In Chapter 17 John's readers share his vision of a woman.
At first glance, she might seem to be the goddess Roma, in
all her glory, a stunning personification of the civilisation of
Rome, as she was worshipped in many a temple in the
cities of Asia. But as John sees her, she is a Roman prostitute,
a seductive whore and a scheming witch, and her wealth
and splendour represent the profits of her disreputable
trade. For good measure there are biblical overtones of the
harlot queen Jezebel to reinforce the impression. In this
way, John's readers are able to to perceive something of
Rome's true character – her moral corruption behind the
enticing propagandist illusions of Rome which they constantly encountered in their cities.

The description of the harlot as seated upon many
waters is also a motif from the prophets. Jeremiah spoke of
Babylon as 'you who dwell by many waters' (51:13). The
allusion is to the Euphrates and the many canals surrounding
the ancient city of Babylon. The prophet Nahum, in
describing the Egyptian city of Thebes, shows that such a
location was a sign of strength – 'with water around her,
her rampart a sea, and water her wall' (Nahum 3:8). The
description does not at all fit the city of Rome. It is taken
over to show that Rome is the new Babylon. A new meaning
is given to the phrase in verse 15: the waters are nations,
people, races, and languages. Rome's strength is symbolised
by the peoples subject to its rule.

Several other remarks show that 'Babylon' is a veiled reference to Rome. The name written on her forehead, The Great Babylon has a secret meaning. The implication is that the name 'Babylon' should not be taken at face value. Later, the seven heads are interpreted as seven mountains on which the woman is seated. This alludes to the seven hills of Rome. The vision closes with a final hint – the woman you saw is the great city that rules over the kings of the earth. The most obvious candidate for this title in John's time was the mighty, imperial city of Rome.

The clothing of the woman – purple and scarlet – symbolises a life of luxury. Her adornment – gold ornaments, precious stones, and pearls – represents the wiles of a woman who wishes to seduce a man who is not her husband.

Throughout the vision, images of harlotry and fornication are used to represent the idea of idolatry. Rome's idolatry consisted in its arrogant pride in its accomplishments, its excessive claims of allegiance and praise, and its illusion of complete autonomy. In Chapter 13, the emphasis was on the beasts' relationship to the creator and to the faithful. Here, Rome's role in the civilisation of the Mediterranean world is emphasised. Rome is depicted as a harlot because she seduced many of the local rulers and ordinary people into accepting her illusory and exaggerated view of her own importance.

From *The Theology of the Book of Revelation*, Cambridge University Press, 1993, (1st paragraph only) and *The Apocalypse*, Veritas, Dublin, 1979, (last 4 paragraphs). Used by kind permission of the publishers.

Saturday of the fourth week of Easter

The Fall of Babylon
Richard Bauckham

It would be a mistake to understand the images of
Revelation as timeless symbols. Their character conforms to
the contextuality of Revelation as a letter to the seven
churches of Asia. Their resonances in the specific social,
political, cultural and religious world of their first readers
need to be understood if their meaning is to be appropriated
today. They do not create a purely self-contained aesthetic
world with no reference outside itself, but intend to relate
to the world in which the readers live in order to reform
and to redirect the readers' response to that world.
However, if the images are not timeless symbols, but relate
to the 'real' world, we need also to avoid the opposite mistake
of taking them too literally as descriptive of the 'real' world
and of predicted events in the 'real' world. They are not just
a system of codes waiting to be translated into matter-of-fact
references to people and events. Once we begin to appreciate
their sources and their rich symbolic associations, we realise
that they cannot be read either as literal descriptions or as
encoded literal descriptions, but must be read for their
theological meaning and their power to evoke response.

Consider, for instance, that the last of the seven Bowls
in Chapter 16 results in the fall of Babylon in an earthquake
of unprecedented proportions. If we took this as literal
prediction we should find it contradicted by later images of
the downfall of Babylon. In Chapter 17 Babylon, now
portrayed as a harlot, is stripped, devoured and burned by

the beast and the ten kings. The traditional punishment of a harlot is here superimposed on the image of a city sacked and razed to the ground by an army. Chapter 18 extends the image of a city beseiged and burned to the ground, but we are told both that the site of the city becomes the haunt of the desert creatures and that the smoke from her burning continues to ascend forever. On the literal level, these images are quite inconsistent with each other, but on the level of theological meaning, conveyed by the allusions to the Old Testament and to contemporary myth, they offer complementary perspectives on the meaning of Babylon's fall. The earthquake is that which accompanies the theophany of the holy God coming to final judgement. The sacking of Babylon by the beast and his allies alludes to the contemporary myth of the return of Nero to destroy Rome. It is an image of the self-destructive nature of evil, which on the level of theological meaning is not inconsistent with the idea of the destruction of evil by divine judgement, but presented under another aspect.

From *The Theology of the Book of Revelation*, Cambridge University Press, 1993. Used by kind permission of the publisher.

Fifth Sunday of Easter

The Way, The Truth, & The Life
Hans Urs von Balthasar

In a world without beauty, the good also loses its radiance. So, what is that 'radiance from within' which makes something 'beautiful', which makes this particular shape or form beautiful, while this other one is not? What is this inner shining that makes something beautiful, loveable, desirable – the inner quality of things that might be called 'splendour'? What happens to the shape or the form of a many-splendoured thing that makes it worthy of our love?

This goes for people too. What is a person without the form that gives them shape, that surrounds them like a suit of armour and yet is the very thing that allows for suppleness and musicality of movement? What is a person without the backbone that gives both flexibility and fragility? What is any one of us without this? Without the form into which we pour our lives, so that our life becomes the pulse and soul of that form, which is us?

It is from such a standpoint that we can understand the gospel which has just been read. Jesus is the way, the 'form' of divine revelation in history. Jesus is the Word, the Image, the Expression, the Exegesis of God. 'Whoever has seen me, has seen the Father.' Jesus shows us who God is through every available means of human expression at his disposal from his birth to his death. These include each age and stage of his life from childhood to adulthood, every social occasion and each solitary situation. He is always the definitive embodiment of God, without being the one to whom this gives definitive expression, namely the Father. Such is the paradox at the origin of the Christian aesthetic.

Only something that has a form can ravish us with beauty. And only through a shape or a form can eternal beauty flash through our world like lightning. And to be bowled over by such an appearance is what happened at the beginning of Christianity. The apostles were captivated by what they saw, heard, and touched, by what was revealed to them in human form. St John above all, but not just he alone, never stops trying to describe how the features of Christ appeared when you met him, whenever you talked with him: the precise way in which the contours of his form were fashioned so that suddenly a shaft of light flashed through this man, in an unaccountable way that would fling you on your knees in adoration and compel you to become his disciple.

Would it not have been cowardly flight to have left everything and followed Jesus if you had not been overcome by that divine madness which even Plato knew in his own way? Each one of us must experience this in our own way, if we are to allow ourselves to become lovers of such beauty of the highest sort. Those of us who have been affected by beauty of any kind in some intimate place within ourselves, whether beauty of nature, of another human being, or in a work of art of whatever kind, will know what such beauty can mean. Such beauty is recognised immediately and its touch is its own proof.

From *The Glory of the Lord Volume I: Seeing the Form*, T.& T. Clark, Edinburgh, 1982 (synopsised). Used by kind permission of Continuum International Publishing Group Ltd.

Monday of the fifth week of Easter

'Fear not and be not dismayed;
the battle is not yours but God's'
Martin Buber

The prophet, like most of us at certain times in our lives, must hear the message, stark and untransfigured, which is delivered out of this biographical and historical hour. Nor must we translate for ourselves its wild and crude profaneness into the chastely religious: each one of us must recognise that the question put to us is God's question to us. It is a question wondrously tuned in the wild crude sound. And we must answer by what we do and do not do. Reduction is forbidden; you are not at liberty to select what suits you, the whole cruel hour claims you and you must answer – God. Let no one interfere; let no one prompt you; give the answer from the depths.

The relationship of faith is no book of rules which can be looked up to discover what is to be done now, in this very hour. I experience what God desires of me not earlier than in this hour. And even then it is not given to me to experience it except by answering before God for this hour as my hour, by carrying out the responsibility for it towards God as much as I can. What has now approached me, the unforeseen, the unforeseeable, is word from him, a word found in no dictionary, a word that has now become word – and it demands my answer to him.

The human person belongs, whether they want to acknowledge it and take it seriously or not, to the community in which they are born or which they happened to get into. For the one living in community, the ground of personal and essential decision is continually threatened by so-called collective decisions. It must be added that the community does not usually express in a unified and unambiguous way what it considers to be right or not right in any given situation. There are usually groups, each knowing what benefits the community and each claiming your unreserved complicity for the good of the community.

My community cannot relieve me of my responsibility for my hour of decision; I must not let it do so. It is not as though they don't concern me in my decision, but no programme, no tactical resolution, no command can tell me how I, as I decide, have to do justice to my community before the face of God. It could be that I must be set in cruel opposition to its success, because God's love ordains otherwise. Only one thing matters: that as the situation is presented to me I expose myself to it, to the very ground where hearing passes into being, that I perceive what is to be perceived and answer it.

From *Between Man and Man*, Collins, Fontana Library, London, 1961. Used by kind permission of the publisher.

Tuesday of the fifth week of Easter

The Dragon
D. H. Lawrence

The woman is one of the 'wonders'. And the other wonder
is the Dragon. The Dragon is one of the oldest symbols of
the human consciousness. The dragon and the serpent
symbol goes so deep in every human consciousness, that a
rustle in the grass can startle the toughest 'modern' to
depths we have no control over.

First and foremost, the dragon is the symbol of the fluid,
rapid, startling movement of life within us. That startled life
which runs through us like a serpent, or coils within us
potent and waiting, like a serpent, this is the dragon. And
the same with the cosmos.

From earliest times, humans have been aware of a
'power' or potency within themselves – and also outside –
over which they have no ultimate control. It is a fluid, rippling
potency which can lie quite dormant, sleeping, and yet be
ready to leap out unexpectedly. Such are the sudden angers
that spring upon us from within ourselves, passionate and
terrible in passionate people: and the sudden excesses of
violent desire, wild sexual desire, or violent hunger, or a
great desire of any sort, even for sleep. The hunger which
made Esau sell his birthright would have been called his
dragon: later, the Greeks would even have called it a 'God'
in him. It is something beyond him, yet within him. It is
swift and surprising as a serpent, and overmastering as a
dragon. It leaps up from somewhere inside him, and has the
better of him.

Primitive humanity, or shall we say early humanity was in a certain sense afraid of its own nature, it was so violent and unexpected inside them. Sometimes it came upon them like a glory, as when Samson slew the lion with his hands, and David slew Goliath with a pebble.

The usual vision of the dragon is, however, not personal but cosmic. It is in the vast cosmos of the stars that the dragon writes and lashes. We see him in his maleficent aspect, red. But don't let us forget that when he stirs green and flashing on a pure dark night of stars it is he who makes the wonder of the night, it is the full rich coiling of his folds which makes the heavens sumptuously serene, as he glides around and guards the immunity, the precious strength of the planets, and gives lustre and new strength to the fixed stars, and still more serene beauty to the moon. His coils within the sun make the sun glad, till the sun dances in radiance. For in his good aspect, the dragon is the great vivifier, the great enhancer of the whole universe.

So he persists still to the Chinese. Proud and strong and grand is the mandarin who is within the folds of the green dragon, lord of the dragon. It is the same dragon which, according to the Hindus, coils quiescent at the base of the spine, and unfolds sometimes lashing along the spinal way: and the yogi is only trying to set this dragon in controlled motion.

From *The Apocalypse,* Penguin Books, London, 1995. Reproduced by permission of Pollinger Limited and the Estate of Frieda Lawrence Ravagli.

Wednesday of the fifth week of Easter

The Temple of the Lord
Yves Congar

Two closely connected dogmas are the fundamental determinants of Israel's religion, namely the oneness and the absoluteness of God and God's choice of Israel to be his own particular people. Jerusalem and, in Jerusalem, the Temple, were the place in which these two combined realities, Yahweh and his people, met in a special manner and in the most complete and intimate union. The fact that the restoration of Ezras and Nehemiah was strictly Judean in character is important and significant. The Jewish community after the exile desired to be segregated and pure, with the Temple as its centre, and so in ascending order from the Jew of the townships of Juda and Benjamin to those of the holy city, to the court of its Temple, the sanctuary and finally the Holy of Holies which the high priest alone entered once a year, it aimed to achieve a type of 'sanctity' that became increasingly strict and increasingly narrow.

We might call this an ontological sanctity, which from its supreme realisation in the Divine Presence in the Holy of Holies, was communicated almost physically to the sanctuary, the priest's court, the women's court, the whole of the sacred area, then to Jerusalem and to the whole of Israel.

We must not, in the name of a spiritual doctrine which also has its perils, fail to recognise the religious nobility of the ritual code and the insistence on legal purity with which the gospel has made us only too familiar solely in its pharisaical and exaggerated forms. The theme of the Temple always accompanied an insistence on purity. In Judaism, it acquired an excessively ritualistic aspect, but it had a religious depth which the story of the Macabees powerfully illustrates. The whole of the national life was marked by it. Postexilic Israel no longer had a king, and it eventually became fully conscious that it did not wish to have one, but only a body of clergy and a high priest, a hierarchy to teach it the Law and to celebrate public worship. The Law and public worship were the two poles, both on the religious and national level, of the life of this separatist Israel. The relationship between the Jewish soul and God was never confined to the sphere of ideas and intentions, it was always operative within the sphere of action, it always desired to be translated into practice not only of an ethical but also of a liturgical type. And in the life of the Jews, as it took shape after the return from exile, the practice of public worship was closely oriented towards and bound up with the Temple.

From *The Mystery of the Temple*, Burns & Oates, London, 1962. Used by kind permission of Continuum International Publishing Group Ltd.

Thursday of the fifth week of Easter

The Holy City
Northrop Frye

Urban imagery is naturally focused on Jerusalem, and cities are apt to be symbolically female, as the word 'metropolis' (mother city) reminds us. In sexual imagery the relation of male to female is expressed in two ways, depending on whether the two bodies or only the sexual organs themselves are taken as the basis. In one the male is above and the female below; in the other the male is at the centre and the female surrounds him. No general trend is without many exceptions in mythology, but throughout Mediterranean and Near Eastern countries, apart from Egypt, there was a general tendency to associate the sky with a male principle and the earth with a female one. The metaphorical kernels of the all-male Christian Trinity of Father, Son, and Spirit are probably the sky, the sun and the air. The other relation is illustrated by the temple of the (usually male) god in the midst of the bridal city. The Jerusalem Temple (at least the typological use made of it in the New Testament, more particularly in the epistle to the Hebrews) had an outer court that was a marketplace, an inner court where the believers gathered, and the inmost Holy of Holies, a space representing the presence of God, covered with a veil and entered once a year by the High Priest. The sacrilege of placing a statue or altar of a heathen god in the temple found its apocalyptic opposite in the coming of a visible God in the flesh. Hence at Jesus' death the veil of the Temple of Jerusalem was torn from top to bottom; Jesus is said by Paul to have broken down the middle wall of partition (Ephesians 2:14); and his act of cleansing the outer temple is of such symbolic importance that John places it at the very beginning of his ministry.

The typical healing act of Jesus is the casting of 'devils' out of the bodies of those possessed by them. As each body is a temple of God (1 Cor 3:16), the casting out of devils is symbolically the same act as cleansing the temple. The process is completed in the apocalypse: the author of Revelation is emphatic that there is no temple in the new Jerusalem, as the body of Christ has replaced it (Rev 21:22). The final consummation of Bridegroom and Bride is thus a total mingling of bodies, and is no longer symbolised, as Blake remarked, by 'a pompous high priest entering by a secret place.' Within the same metaphorical construct, Christ is not only the temple but the cornerstone of the temple, and each member of the Christian community is a stone in the same temple.

From *The Great Code, The Bible and Literature*, Ark Paperbacks, an imprint of Routledge & Kegan Paul, London, 1982.

Friday of the fifth week of Easter

Real Presence
Yves Congar

The prophets' mission was to throw light upon and also to further the realisation of God's plan which, by successive stages, was moving towards its final consummation in Jesus Christ. They were to prevent this movement from a fixation at one or other of its stages or in one or other of its characteristics. This was their duty particularly after the building of the Temple by Solomon. People were not to think, as Solomon himself was inclined to do, that God's purpose had been fulfilled, the promise to David accomplished, and that the Temple with its priesthood and worship now represented the very truth of the Presence. This was a genuine danger and Judaism succumbed to it when, after the restoration of Esdras and Zorobabel, the voice of the great prophets was silent. This is why the prophets continued to emphasise the dual nature of the Israelite theology of the Presence, the tension between the assertion of a Presence linked with the holy place and the tabernacle, and the assertion of the existence of a transcendent Yahweh, dwelling in heaven and bringing his action to bear in every place. In the forefront of the prophets' teaching there is always testimony to a tension between Sion and the Temple, the place of God's presence, and the reality of Yahweh himself, the transcendent, living and active God who alone is genuine Presence.

Above all, this is why the prophets make two opposing assertions concerning the Temple, just as they do in the case of sacrifices, the Sabbath and feasts. In one of the greatest passages in the whole of Christian literature, St Augustine has clearly shown the pattern of this dialectic of Sacrifice: 'Let us see how when God says he wants no sacrifice, he makes it clear that there is one he does want. God does not want the sacrifice of slaughtered beasts, he wants the sacrifice of a broken heart.' The prophets say: 'God wants no sacrifices, your ceremonies fill him with loathing!' Yet elsewhere they say that he wants them more than ever! He does and yet does not want them. He wants sacrifices but not of the kind that are offered to him. And the reason for his refusal is to be sought at a far deeper level than the moral obliquities which in fact accompany the offering of sacrifices. True, the prophets frequently condemn these misdeeds and in terms on which we can never meditate enough, but they are not moral reformers, they are much more than that. Just as Jesus, when he drove the buyers and sellers from the Temple, was not merely insisting on the moral conduct required within the sacred place but on something far more important. His gesture was prophetic and inaugurated a new stage in the accomplishment of the mystery of the Temple. It was the prophets' mission to foretell this stage. This is the point of their dialectic, asserting as it does two truths: there is no Presence (of the kind you know and are so anxious to preserve); and God will be present more than ever before. There will be a new Temple and God will be for ever with his people.

From *The Mystery of the Temple*, Burns & Oates, London, 1962. Used by kind permission of Continuum International Publishing Group Ltd.

Saturday of the fifth week of Easter

Early Christian Worship
Oscar Cullmann

Our sources for the investigation of the early Christian service of worship do not yield a perfectly clear picture of the outward development of the gatherings for worship; they do disclose, however, a fairly clear tendency in worship.

What then are the essential component parts of the service of worship celebrated in these gatherings? First of all we are bound to say that they are extraordinarily manifold and that the worship life of our church in contrast seems remarkably impaired. In the Book of Acts, instruction, preaching, prayer and breaking of bread are mentioned, and mentioned in such a way as clearly to show that these elements were, from the beginning, the foundation of all the worship life of the Christian community.

For the oldest liturgical prayers, however, we must go to the prayer preserved in the Aramaic *Maranatha*: 'Come Lord Jesus.' The Greek translation at the end of the Book of Revelation (22:20) shows that *Maranatha* is an imperative, that is to say a prayer, and not an indicative: 'Our Lord is coming.' This call in prayer stands in the Aramaic form at the end of the Epistle to the Corinthians (16:22). From the *Didache* we discover that it was said in particular at the end of the meal in connection with the eucharistic liturgy. The fact that this prayer is handed down by Paul untranslated and that it continued in that original form until the time of the composition of the *Didache* shows the extraordinarily important rôle which this oldest liturgical prayer of the early Christian community must have played. The *Didache* has handed down to us other eucharistic prayers which have almost word for word parallels in Judaism. In the *Maranatha* prayer, on the other hand, we come right down to the specifically Christian element in early liturgical prayer, an element which connects closely with the fact that the day of the Christian service of worship is the day of Christ's resurrection. On this day Christ appeared at a meal with the disciples. So now he ought to appear again, in the Christian celebration of the Meal, since, 'where two or three are gathered together in my name, there am I in the midst of them' (Mt 18:20). This presence of the Spirit in the congregation is, however, an earnest of his coming at the End. This ancient prayer thus points at the same time backwards to Christ's appearance on the day of his resurrection, to his present appearance at the common meal of the community and forwards to his appearance at the End, which is often represented by the picture of a Messianic meal. In all three cases a meal is involved. Therefore the *Maranatha* is above all a eucharistic prayer.

From *Early Christian Worship*, SCM Press, London, 1953. Used by kind permission of the publisher.

Sixth Sunday of Easter

The Absences of Jesus
Hans Urs von Balthasar

For human thought, and still more for human feeling and experience, God's presence and absence in the world are an unsearchable mystery. In human form, the Son has 'made known' the Father, whom no one had ever seen; as the incarnate Word, he clothed the ineffable in human categories, in such a way that in things that are comprehensible to us, the essentially incomprehensible God shines through. Jesus would not have revealed the Father to us as his Word, had he brought only his immanence and not his transcendence. Jesus has to teach us that 'in him we see our God made visible and so are caught up in love of the God we cannot see' (*Christmas Preface*). This becomes manifest in the manner in which Jesus' permanent state of being with us is realised by means of increasingly pronounced withdrawals and absences. It would almost seem that his coming into the world was merely the occasion for his disappearance: 'Now I leave the world and go to the Father' (Jn 16:28). But this 'going to the Father' is the very manner of his returning or remaining. 'You heard me say to you: I am going away and shall return to you. If you loved me you would be glad that I am going to the Father' (Jn 14:28). There are two reasons for this: The first is added to the same sentence: 'For the Father is greater than I.' In Jesus' disappearing to go to the greater God, he enters into his own proper form, which was prefigured on the Mount of Transfiguration and became definitive for him at the Resurrection. The disciples must show the genuineness of their love by allowing him this form in place of that transient, material one which he had assumed for love of them and in which they experience him as present. The other reason is expressed in the statement: 'I am telling you the truth: it is for your good that I am going, for unless I go, the Paraclete will not come to you; but if I do go, I will send him to you' (Jn 16:7). This means that this last indicated presence of God, the Spirit of the Father and of the Son, can become a reality only in the Son's withdrawal of his physical presence, and indeed only in its being accepted by each one of us.

From *New Elucidations*, Ignatius Press, San Francisco, 1986. Used by kind permission of the publisher.

Monday of the sixth week of Easter

Christi Manifested in Remembrance
John Henry Newman

When our Lord was leaving his apostles, and they were sorrowful, he consoled them by the promise of another Guide and Teacher, on whom they might rely instead of him, and who should be more to them even than he had been. He promised them the Third Person in the Ever-blessed Trinity, the Spirit of himself and of his Father, who should come invisibly. His presence would be more real and efficacious by how much it was more secret and inscrutable. At the same time, this new and most gracious Comforter would not in any degree obscure or hide what had gone before. Though he did more for the apostles than Christ had done, he would not throw into the shade and super-sede him whom he succeeded. On the contrary, Christ expressly announced: 'He shall glorify me.'

The special way in which God the Holy Spirit gave glory to God the Son, seems to have been his revealing him as the Only-begotten Son of the Father, who had appeared as the Son of man. Apparently, it was not till after his resur-rection, and especially after his ascension, when the Holy Spirit descended, that the apostles understood who had been with them. When all was over they knew it, not at the time.

Now here we see, I think, the trace of a general principle, which comes before us again and again both in scripture and in the world, that God's Presence is not discerned at the time when it is upon us, but afterwards, when we look back upon what is gone and over.

Look back upon your past life, and you will find how critical were moments and acts, which at the time seemed the most indifferent: as for instance, the school you were sent to as a child, the occasion of your falling in with those persons who have most benefited you, the accidents which determined your calling or prospects whatever they were. The most ordinary years, when we seemed to be living for nothing, these shine forth to us in their very regularity and orderly course. The planting of Christ's Cross in the heart is sharp and trying; but the stately tree rears itself aloft, and has fair branches and rich fruit, and is good to look upon. At the time, we cannot realise, we can but believe that Christ is with us; but after an interval a sweetness breathes from them, as from his garments, 'of myrrh, aloes, and cassia'.

We come, like Jacob, in the dark, and lie down with a stone for our pillow; but when we rise again, and call to mind what has passed, we recollect we have seen a vision of angels. What is dark while it is meeting us, reflects the Sun of Righteousness when it is past. Let us profit by this in future, so far as this, to have faith in what we cannot see. The Presence of the Eternal Son, ten times more glorious, more powerful than when he trod the earth in our flesh, is with us. Let us ever bear in mind this divine truth – the more secret God's hand is, the more powerful. He who glorified Christ, imparts him thus glorified to us.

From *Parochial and Plain Sermons*, Vol Sermon 16.

Tuesday of the sixth week of Easter

Liturgy and the Movement of the Spirit
J. D. Crichton

The liturgy is a manifestation of the Spirit and the principal means in the church by which the Holy Spirit is communicated. This may seem surprising to some, possibly because the presence of the Spirit was not prominent in the former liturgy, but also because the action of the Holy Spirit in the church and in individuals has been until recently largely ignored by western Christians.

The presence and action of the Holy Spirit are made plain over the wole range of the sacraments of initiation. At the Easter Vigil, when candidates are to be baptised, the celebrant plunges the lighted paschal candle into the water singing, 'We ask you Father, with your Son, to send the Holy Spirit upon the waters of this font …' The comprehensive nature of the action of the Spirit in the eucharist is made clearest in the fourth eucharistic prayer where we pray: 'Look upon this sacrifice which you have given to your church and by your Holy Spirit gather all who share this bread and this cup into the one body of Christ, a living sacrifice of praise.' Here the ascending movement of the eucharist, the offering, and the descending movement, the coming of the Spirit on the people gathering them into one body is made plain. The Holy Spirit is active throughout the whole eucharistic action.

While all this is true it seems that even now the structures of the liturgy are inhibiting the manifestations of the Spirit and sometimes the manner of celebration makes these impossible. The stream of words, which might be described as the stream of unconsciousness, that washes over the heads of the people is not conducive to the movement of the soul that it may make contact with and respond to the Holy Spirit who is given thoughout the service. It is for this reason that the silences suggested by the new Order of Mass are important. The Holy Spirit can and does speak in the silence of the heart.

From *The Once and the Future Liturgy*, Veritas, Dublin, 1977. Used by kind permission of the publisher.

Wednesday of the sixth week of Easter

Between Time and Eternity
Romano Guardini

The days between Christ's Resurrection and his return to the Father are full of mystery. If we accept them as we should, not as a legend, but as a vital part of our faith, then we must ask what they mean in the life of the Lord, and what their significance is in our own Christian existence.

These are the days between time and eternity. The Lord is still on earth, but his feet are already detached, prepared to depart. In the New Testament there are two figures of Jesus; one 'the carpenter's son' who stands in the midst of earthly events, who toils, struggles, submits to his destiny. He has his own personal characteristics – mysterious and inexplicable, certainly – and yet so unmistably his that we almost hear the tone of his voice, see the accompanying gesture. In the main, it is the gospels that portray this Son of Man.

The other 'nature' of Jesus is centred in eternity. Here all earthly limitations have fallen away. Nothing transitory, nothing accidental remains; everything is essence. 'Jesus of Nazareth' has become 'Christ our Lord', the eternal one whose figure St John describes as it was revealed to him on the Island of Patmos: 'One like to a son of man, clothed with a garment reaching to his ankles, and a gold band around his chest. His hair was white as wool, or as snow, and his eyes blazed like fire. And out of his mouth came a sharp two-edged sword; and his face was like the sun shining in its power.

And when I saw him, I fell at his feet as one dead. And he laid his right hand upon me, saying, "Do not be afraid; I am the First and the Last, and the living one; I was dead, and behold, I am alive forevermore; and I have the keys of death and of hell".'

St Paul also describes him in the epistle to the Colossians as 'the image of the invisible God, the first-born of every creature. For in him were created all things in the heavens and on the earth, things visible and things invisible, whether Thrones, or Dominations, or Principalities, or Powers … For it has pleased God the Father that in him all his fullness should dwell.'

Here all concrete detail falls away. Not one familiar trait remains; hardly a human feature. Everything is strange and disproportionate. Is it the same Jesus who walked on earth? The days we are speaking of reply. Those few days of transition from time to eternity prove that he is one and the same here as well as there; that when Jesus of Nazareth entered 'into his glory,' he took with him his whole earthly existence, which continues to live in 'Alpha and the Omega, the beginning and the end … who is who was and who is to come, the Almighty.'

From *The Lord*, Longmans, Green & Co, London, 1956.

Thursday of the sixth week of Easter

Why the Ascension?
Romano Guardini

It might be asked: Why this mysterious lingering on earth after the Resurrection? Why didn't the Lord return home directly? What was happening during those forty days?

Let us for a moment suppose that the Resurrection and the period afterwards had been mere offshoots of morbid religious experience, legend or myth – what would those days have looked like? Doubtless, they would have been filled with demonstrations of the liberated one's power; the hunted one, now omnipotent, would have shattered his enemies; he would have blazed from temple altars, would have covered his followers with honours, and in these and other ways, would have fulfilled the longings of the oppressed. He would also have initiated the disciples into the wonderful mysteries of heaven, would have revealed the future, the beginning and end of all things. But nothing of this occurs. No mysteries are revealed; no one is initiated into the secrets of the unknown. What does happen? Something completely unspectacular, delicately still: the past is confirmed. The reality of the life that has been crosses over into eternity. These days are the period of that transition.

And we need them for our faith; particularly when we evoke the great images of the eternal Christ throning at his Father's right, coming upon the clouds to judge the living and the dead. Such images place us in danger of losing the earthly figure of the Lord. This must not happen. Everything depends on the eternal Christ's remaining also

Jesus of Nazareth, who walks among us until the day when all things will be enfolded in eternity; on the blending of the borderless spirit with the here and now and then of the process of salvation. In the Christ of the Apocalypse one vision holds this fast: the Lamb standing 'as if slain' but alive. Earthly destiny entered into eternity. Once and forever, death has become lasting life. But there is a danger that this truth dangle in space, enigmatic as a rune on an ancient stone. This period of transition deciphers the rune, gives us the key: all that has been remains in eternal form. Every word Jesus ever spoke, every event during his lifetime is fixed in unchanging reality, then and now and forever. He who is seated on the throne contains the past transfigured to eternal present.

From *The Lord*, Longmans, Green & Co, London, 1956.

Friday of the sixth week of Easter

The Departures of Jesus
Hans Urs von Balthasar

The departure of Jesus, announced but not understood, can at first only be misinterpreted: 'Is he going to kill himself, since he says "Where I am going, you cannot come"?' (Jn 8:22). The apostles, too, hear him announce his going, but since they have his earthly presence in mind, they cannot grasp it. They either naïvely declare their willingness to die with him (that is, their unwillingness to allow the intended separation to take place); or they assert their intention to remain with him in any event; or they ask where he is going, so that they can go along. But for the time being they receive the answer: 'Little children, I shall be with you only a little longer. You will look for me, but where I am going, you cannot come.'

The distance between heaven and earth always remains. On the whole, Jesus' experienced presence is merely the means and the point of departure for setting the believing church in motion on her incalculably long, seemingly lonely journey through time. 'Happy are they who do not see and yet believe' (Jn 20:29). This relationship in faith had to be practised also throughout Jesus' entire earthly life, so full of partings, separations and withdrawals, both outwardly and inwardly. Even where Jesus' presence is publicly proclaimed he is essentially unrecognised: 'There stands among you one whom you do not know' (Jn 1:26). John the Baptist himself did not know him until the sign appeared. This strangeness that characterises his presence makes him seem absent even where he is present: he goes up to the festival 'not openly, but as if secretly'. 'At the festival the Jews were looking for him and asking, "Where is he?"' (Jn 7:11). His seemingly impossible presence is veiled in mystery and appears as absence. The faith of his disciples is equally insufficient to recognise him as the one walking towards them on the water at night. They cry out in terror, because 'they thought it was a ghost' (Mk 6:49). This holds true to the end: 'I have been with you all this time, and still you do not know me?' (Jn 14:9).

His presence, misunderstood and not benefited from, is the time of salvation granted by God, but as a 'little while'. The expression 'little while' becomes a kind of secret key to Jesus' whole way of existence in his earthly life and in his Passion. '"In a little while you will no longer see me, and then a little while later you will see me again." At this some of his disciples said to one another, "What does he mean in telling us: In a little while you will no longer see me, and then a little while later you will see me again?" They kept asking, "What is this 'little while'? We don't know what he is talking about".' In this key passage two things interpenetrate: the economy of the grace bestowed from above, allowing the invisible to become visible for a short time, and the counter-economy of sin that refuses to see what is shown and drives it away into invisibility and absence.

From *New Elucidations*, Ignatius Press, San Francisco, 1986. Used by kind permission of the publisher.

Saturday of the sixth week of Easter

Does The World Hate You?
Karl Rahner

'You must not be surprised when the world hates you.' If we look at the context of this verse, we find the following: 'We are to love one another; not to be like Cain, who belonged to the Evil One and cut his brother's throat.' We must not be people who hate others because we cannot endure goodness. According to John love, kindness, holiness, and justice arouse hatred. He assumes that Christians are people who do good works, like Abel. So John thinks that goodness and justice provoke the antagonism, anger, and hatred of the unjust because they cannot endure the contrast with themselves; they want to see their actions endorsed by the actions of others, and they are forced to blame themselves and disavow their actions if they meet someone else whose deeds are just and good, even to the point of loving their evil attackers. So goodness stirs up malice, love stirs up hatred, and justice injustice. Injustice comes to light and is exposed because it cannot bear goodness. Now John says that this must happen to us; he admonishes us not to be surprised when it does happen to us.

Let us be perfectly frank. Can we say that the world hates us? Do we suffer violence and impoverishment for conscience' sake? To be honest we are no better off than many other countries, we have our difficulties and perhaps our tragedies, but we cannot really pretend that the world hates us because we are just, because we love those who hate us. Now if such is the case, are we really what we should be, people that St John can assume will be hated by the world and who must be admonished not to wonder at that hatred? By this standard of real Christianity we may well find ourselves wanting before God and our conscience.

We need the light of God, a fidelity and a purity of conscience that is able to criticise ourselves and criticise the world. A staggering task. We must keep asking ourselves whether we are not, in St Paul's phrase, too much conformed to this world. We must keep asking whether we do not misrepresent Christianity and give scandal to those who are in search of true Christianity, because we pretend to be Christians and are nothing of the kind. May God give us the grace to bear the real hatred of the world with courage and equanimity; and may God give the church of today and her hierarchy, and each one of us in our own lives, the grace not to make Christianity seem to the world unworthy of credence through our own fault.

From *Biblical Homilies*, Herder & Herder, London, 1966.

Seventh Sunday of Easter

Love Alone: The Way of Revelation
Hans Urs von Balthasar

Christian love is not the world's last word about itself – it is
God's final word about himself, and so about the world. In
the Cross we see, above all, something foreign to the world,
something which cuts clean across worldly understanding.
For the world wants to live and rise again without dying;
but Christ's love wishes to die, in order that, through death,
it may rise again beyond death in God's form.

If the Cross is turned into a law which reason can grasp
and administer, even an elastic sort of law governing the
rhythm of life, then it is once again a law – in the Pauline
sense – and absolute love is displaced and set aside by
knowledge: which means to say that God's sovereign freedom
is judged before the court of human reason – and condemned
as that which it really is.

There is a genuine knowledge regarding faith which is
the 'gnosis' so constantly stressed in the gospels; it is possible
to reflect upon ourselves and upon our world in the light
of the knowledge of faith and discover the watermark of
God's love in individual natures and in nature as a whole.
But this sign, impressed upon nature, first comes to light
when the sign of absolute love has appeared: then the being
of the world can be interpreted in the light of the cross; the
inchoate forms and ways of love, which otherwise threaten
to lead nowhere, can be elucidated in their proper
transcendental setting.

The values of this world are only set in a true light

when seen in relation to God's sign, because then the limits of love, the obstacles to it, are overcome, and the mystery of self-sacrificing love is sageguarded against the inroads of knowledge.

And above all, we only become who we really are when addressed in this context: singled out as the person addressed, we become fully ourselves in our response. We are the language God uses to speak to us. How could we possibly not understand ourselves in this langauge? Bathed in the light of God, we step into our own clarity.

In the light of the sign of God who annihilated himself to become man and to die forsaken, it becomes possible to perceive why God came forth from himself and became the creator of the world; expressing his absolute being and revealing as unfathomable love his perfect freedom, which is not an absolute beyond being, but the height, the depth, the length and the breadth of being itself.

From *Love Alone: The Way of Revelation*, Compass Books, London, 1968.

Monday of the seventh week of Easter

The Holy Spirit
Yves Congar

Persons are the great wealth of the church. Each one is an original and autonomous principle of sensitivity, experience, relationships and intiatives. What an infinite variety of possibilities is contained in each individual! There are signs of a purely material kind of this individuality – each person's fingerprints are, for example, distinctive. If it is true that no two trees are identical throughout the whole world, what are we to say about humankind in space and time? And how many languages are there in the world? It has been estimated that there are some 5,000. And in each one the possible expressions and combinations are really infinite. This is a sign of our skill and intelligence and therefore of the number of initiatives open to us.

Individual persons, however, want to be the subjects of their actions. Nothing less than the Spirit of God is needed to bring all these different elements to unity, and to do so by respecting and even stimulating their diversity. The Spirit, who is both one and transcendent, is able to penetrate all things without violating or doing violence to them. It was with good reason that the Book of Wisdom said of the Spirit: 'The Spirit of the Lord has filled the world and that which holds all things together knows what is said' (1:7) and of wisdom itself, which has the same part to play: 'In her there is a spirit that is intelligent, holy, unique, manifold, subtle, mobile, . . . all-powerful, overseeing all and penetrating through all spirits' (7:22-23).

The Spirit, then, is unique and present everywhere, transcendent and inside all things, subtle and sovereign, able to respect freedom and to inspire it. That Spirit can further God's plan, which can be expressed in the words 'communion,' 'many in one,' 'uniplurality'. At the end, there will be a state in which God will be 'everything to everyone' (1 Cor 15:28), in other words, there will be one life animating many without doing violence to the inner experience of anyone, just as, on Mount Sinai, Yahweh set fire to the bush and it was not consumed.

From *I Believe in the Holy Spirit, Vol II: Lord and Giver of Life,* Chapman, London, 1983. Used by kind permission of the publisher.

Tuesday of the seventh week of Easter

The Holy Spirit
Yves Congar

It was the Spirit who sanctified Jesus' humanity from the moment of his conception and at his baptism, through his resurrection and who makes it possible for one Body, which is the Body of Christ, to exist. 'There are varieties of gifts, but the same Spirit (1 Cor 12:4). The Spirit was in Jesus during his life on earth. Since the time of his glorification, the Spirit has been communicated jointly by 'God' and by the Lord in order to form Christ in each believer, and to make all believers, together and with each other, his Body.

The Holy Spirit is the subject who brings about everything that depends on grace, and is, therefore, the supreme and transcendent effective personality of the church. The Holy Spirit is not consubstantial with us. In Christ, on the other hand, the Word, the Son, assumed a humanity that is consubstantial with our humanity. He united it to himself in a unity that is personal and substantial. Since that time, God has ceased to govern creation exclusively from heaven and on the basis of God's divinity – God governs it in and through that man, Jesus Christ, assumed in his glory. The humanity of Christ, made entirely holy by the Spirit, has since then been the voluntary organ of the communication of grace. Christ gives grace, he gives the Spirit voluntarily. Since that time, the Lord Jesus and the Holy Spirit have together been the authors of the Body, in other words, of the church in its unity.

From *I Believe in the Holy Spirit, Vol II: Lord and Giver of Life*, Chapman, London, 1983. Used by kind permission of the publisher.

Wednesday of the seventh week of Easter

The Filioque
Jean-Miguel Garrigues

Both the Greek and the Latin traditions in the church have developed, each in their own way, one of the irreducible and yet inseparable aspects of the mysterious abyss which is the Father in our trinitarian faith. The Greeks promoted the incommunicable reality of the Godhead, the Person of the Father as unique origin of both the Son and the Holy Spirit. The Latins, on the other hand, expressed the communicable aspect of the Godhead with the Father as source of consubstantial communion and principle of trinitarian order.

However, the truth is that the Father is both of these realities: at one and the same time, he is the origin of the irreducible diversity of personhood within the trinity, while at the same time he is the divine source of that self-communication which maintains the consubstantial communion of all three persons of the Trinity. By opposing these two inseparable dimensions of the mystery of the Father, the two traditions of East and West have ended up through their ecclesial dysfunctionality by obscuring the most intimate and mysterious reality of the 'bosom of the Father' which is, of course, *agape* or love. In fact, it is true to say that there never has been a truly ecumenical acceptation of the full dogma of the Holy Spirit in our churches. At the end of the 4th century the churches of the East and the West professed both the divinity and the personhood of the Holy

Spirit, but each in their own corner and following their own perspectives

From *L'Esprit qui dit "Pere"*, Tequi, Paris, 1981.

Thursday of the seventh week of Easter

Pentecost
Karl Rahner

The centre of all reality, the innermost heart of all infinity, the love of the all-holy God has become our centre, our heart. The only thing that nightfall means now is that we cannot grasp the meaning of the day that has dawned since Pentecost – the day that will see no sunset. The tears of our despair and of our ever-recurring disappointments are nothing but trivial illusions that veil an eternal joy.

God is ours. He has not given us merely a gift, a gift created and finite like ourselves. No, he has given us his whole being without reserve: he has given us the clarity of his knowledge, the freedom of his love, the bliss of his trinitarian life. He has given us himself. And his name is Holy Spirit.

That is the good news of Pentecost, the radiant message, the tidings of strength, light and victory, the message that God loves us and has blessed us with himself. Has that message penetrated our hearts? Is it really there – in the bloodstream – or is it merely stirring rhetoric, pious words for the feast day? Do we not have to cry out with the man in the gospel, 'I believe, Lord, help my unbelief' (Mk 9:24).

Like the wind, the Spirit of God blows where he will, and in his loving patience he roams throughout all the streets of the world in order to touch us there, where we are. And, in the omnipotence of his grace, he may find many to touch. And he says: 'You are mine.' Here God stamps his indestructible seal in our hearts. Here, in the very depths of our being, the Father plants his Holy Spirit, his sacred strength, his divine life. And this has happened to us. We are baptised. God has touched us, not merely by ideas and theories, not merely in pious moods and feelings, but by his own personal, incarnate action, which he works in us in baptism through his ordained servant. We can quench the Spirit, we can hinder him from bringing the fruit of eternal life into us. And that is why we must open ourselves again each day to this Spirit of the Lord, turn to him again each day, be converted to him again each day. Daily conversion requires us also to pray for the Holy Spirit. The church was in prayer when the Holy Spirit came on Pentecost. He is the Spirit of grace that cannot be merited. He is the unfathomable marvel of God's love. Our deeds do not force him down from heaven, nor can the despairing cry of our distress compel him. He is and he remains, always and at each moment, the free gift from above. Come, secret joy, into the tears of the world. We have nothing that can force you; yet on that very account we are confident. *Veni, Sancte Spiritus*.

From *The Eternal Year*, London, Burns & Oates, 1964. Used by kind permission of Continuum International Publishing Group Ltd.

Feast of the Ascension of the Lord

The Ascension
Hans Urs von Balthasar

Luke alone mentions and describes the Ascension of the Lord in the presence of his disciples. In his second work (the Book of the Acts) he dates it as the conclusion of the forty days during which Jesus appeared to his disciples. The concept of a round number here creates no difficulties. It is patterned on the stories of Moses and Elijah, and on Jesus' stay in the desert, and, correspondingly, asks to be understood as a sacred number. The difficulty lies in the representation of an Ascension detached from the Resurrection, and in the meaning to be attached to that special time of the appearances sandwiched between the two.

The self-disclosure of fundamentally transcendent events *vis-à-vis* witnesses in space and time requires not only that free room for manoeuvre which befits the one who reveals himself, but also free room for interpretation into human words and images, for which the interpreter must take responsibility in his own freedom as well as in the obligation incumbent on him to speak out.

Luke's presentation of the mystery takes place in a liturgical setting. The Ascension is described and effected in a blessing: 'And lifting up his hands he blessed them. Now as he blessed them, he withdrew from them' (24:50). This event forms the end of Luke's gospel (24:50-52) and the opening of his second work, The Acts of the Apostles (1:6-11). Christ's leaving us was the necessary preliminary to all future progress in the spiritual life. *Noli me tangere* means stop holding on to my physical presence, my external reality. Find that presence and that strength inside yourself. So his ascending to the right hand of the Father was the blessing he bestowed upon us. Leaving and separation, painful as they might be at the time, are, in fact, the greatest blessing because they allow us to find ourselves, and, more importantly, to receive the Holy Spirit within ourselves. It is only now that the separation is complete, in the view of Luke, that 'the acts of the apostles' can begin. Not just in his second book, but in our own lives. We are the apostles who are asked by the angel interpreters: 'Why are you still looking up into the sky?' He is risen and has gone before you. Wherever you go from now on, God is there before you, and the Holy Spirit is deep within you, acting as your guide.

From *Mysterium Paschale*, T&T Clark, Edinburgh, 1990. Used by kind permission of Continuum International Publishing Group Ltd.

Friday of the seventh week of Easter

The Divine Office and The Holy Spirit
J. D. Crichton

On the assumption that the Divine Office becomes in a
future, near or far, the prayer of a great number of ordinary
people, it will be seen that this is a *kairos*, a privileged
moment for the reception of the Spirit. St Benedict, who in
the sixth century provided the office for all monastic families
of the West, was perfectly well aware of this. Prayer, he says,
should be pure and short 'unless it chance to be prolonged
by the impulse and inspiration of divine grace', that is by
the Holy Spirit. He thought of the calm and orderly
celebration of the prayer as a quietening of the mind and
the senses so that the monk could hear the voice of God in
the psalms and in the readings and the Holy Spirit could
make his presence known. That the revised office makes
this possible can hardly be doubted. The antiphon may be
followed by a silence or there may be one at the end of the
psalm before the psalm-collect, if it is used. Silence is
recommended after the readings in morning or evening
prayer and, of course, may be prolonged if the community
so desires. But perhaps it is the intercessions that offer the
most favourable opportunity for unstructured prayer when
the official prayers have been said. There is no reason why
the prayers of members of the community should not be
uttered aloud. This may not suit all communities but where
'charismatics' gather it would seem right that at least the
first part of their prayer is structured and room left at this
point for unstructured prayer. The community will have

prayed the psalms 'in the Spirit', they will have listened to the reading by which the Holy Spirit is communicated to them, and they will be prepared to respond to the movement of the Spirit. They will, in the words of St Paul, be praying 'not only with the spirit but with the mind as well' (which he considered necessary) and the final result will be that the two forms of prayer, the liturgical and the charismatic, will be combined.

From *The Once and the Future Liturgy*, Veritas, Dublin, 1977. Used by kind permission of the publisher.

Saturday of the seventh week of Easter

The Kenosis of the Spirit
Sergius Bulgakov

The Father reveals himself, not to the world directly but to the Son and Spirit, whereas Son and Spirit are the revelatory persons, emptying themselves into the world to manifest the will of the Father. The whole Trinity, not just the Son, stands in a kenotic relationship with the world, although each Person has its own distinctive mode of *kenosis*, or self-emptying. The *kenosis* of the Father is the creation of the world out of nothing. The act of creation is not just a manifestation of divine might, but a voluntary self-diminishment, a metaphysical *kenosis* whereby the divine Absolute admits the existence of beings outside itself.

The Son reveals himself but conceals his divinity; the Spirit manifests its divinity but conceals itself. The *kenosis* of the Son consists in 'taking the form of a slave, being born in human likeness' (Phil 2:7); the *kenosis* of the Spirit consists in being the servant of the Son and therefore concealing its own identity or 'Face' until the end of the age. The difference in modes should not be taken to imply the *kenosis* of each divine Person takes place in isolation. On the contrary, the Trinity is the quintessential image of communion. So, for example, while the Son and only the Son is sent into the world to die on the cross, both the Father and Spirit participate in the Son's Passion. The father is 'orphaned' by the crucifixion, as is also the Holy Spirit.

The Spirit does not force human freedom but persuades it, winning it over with patience and humility in an 'ongoing Pentecost' or 'final *kenosis*' which will continue until the end of the age.

The Spirit is seen not just as the church-giver on Pentecost, but as the life-giver on the first day, and as the enlivener and beautifier of creation every day. Seen in this perspective, the gift of Pentecost is best described not as new life, which may suggest discontinuity with that which precedes it, but as renewal or 'newness of life,' in the felicitous expression of the Book of Common Prayer. Because the Holy Spirit is the life-giver of both church and world, these two realities must be regarded as ontologically linked, no matter how separate they appear to be in the fallen state of humanity.

From *Modern Russian Theology, Bukharev, Soloviev, Bulgakov, Orthodox Theology in a new key*, T&T Clark, Edinburgh, 2000. Used by kind permission of Continuum International Publishing Group Ltd.

Seven Beams from a Pentecost Novena

Pentecost, 1942
Edith Stein

I. Who are You, sweet light
    That fills up my heart?
    It was once so dark. You hold my hand
    Like a mother and lead me forward.
    I couldn't take a step without You.
    For then my being would return to the void
    That You drew me out of.
    You now form a space inside and about me,
    You are nearer to me than I am to myself,
    Closer to my thoughts than I am.
    But I can't find or touch You
    Because You are beyond names.

       Holy spirit –
          Eternal love!

II. Aren't You the sweet manna
    That pours from the Son's heart into mine?
    Aren't you the food
    For angels and blessed souls?
    Because the one who rose from the dead
    Woke me up to a new world
    And he gives me new life day after day.
    Soon I will be completely filled with his life
    The life of Your life – yes – You yourself.

       Holy spirit –
          Eternal life!

III. Are you the ray
  Of light streaming from the throne of judgement
  Only to break into the dark night
  Of my soul, a soul that never knew itself?
  With mercy but without rest, you enter secret places.
  A soul is afraid to see itself.
  It steps aside to make room for the fear
  Of God and the beginning of wisdom.
  They come down anyway and bind us
  Like anchors to their heights –
  To Your ways that recreate us.

      Holy spirit –
          All-penetrating ray!

IV. Are You the one
  Whose strength and spirit
  Allows the Lamb to loosen the seals
  On the eternal laws of God?
  Messengers of judgement
  Race across the earth driven by You.
  Now your sharp sword divides
  The reign of light from the reign of night
  And the Heavens and earth are made new again
  Through You. Everything finds its rightful place.

      Holy spirit –
          Conquering power!

V. Are You the master-builder of the eternal dome
  That rises all the way from earth to heaven?
  Its columns come alive through You,
  Rise high and stand firm.
  Stamped with God's eternal name

They extend into the light
With a cupola on top
That crowns the dome.
Your work encompasses the whole universe.

> Holy spirit –
> God's shaping hand.

VI Are You the one who made the mirror
That brightens the throne of God
Like a crystal sea
Into which the Godhead looks and loves what he sees?
You bend over your greatest creation
That reflects your own splendour in return.
The beauty of all beings merge there
And become the single form of the virgin.
Your pure bride.

> Holy spirit –
> Creator of the World.

VII. Are You the sweet song of love
And adoration
That rings around the throne of God
And brings together the tone of all beings
Into one thing? Yourself?
This is the harmony that unites body and mind
Until each one finds the secret meaning
Of existence and blissfully releases it
Into the free passage of Your streams.

> Holy spirit –
> Eternal jubilation.

Translated by Fanny Howe.